Heaven's Moon

David T Spofforth

VisionWeaver Press

Published by VisionWeaver Press

Cover painting by David T Spofforth

Typesetting by Riverside Publishing Solutions
www.riversidepublishingsolutions.com

www.heavensmoon.co.uk

Praise for Heaven's Moon

"David's exploration of White Moon Selena draws together strands of thought and belief about the mysterious non-physical Moon, first described in Russian Astrology and connected to Zoroastrianism. This second Moon is said to be a portal to a spiritual moonlight that directs you to the places where your highest aspirations in life may be found. An illuminating guide describing the seven year cycle of this White Moon and its journey through the signs of the Zodiac."

~ Kathy Jones, Priestess of Avalon and Founder of the Glastonbury Goddess Temple
www.kathyjones.co.uk

*

"In this provocative and well-researched book, Spofforth introduces us to the vaguely known White Moon Selena, 'the hypothetical moon', and counterpoint to Black Moon Lilith in astrology. Through Spofforth's shared information, we learn that White Moon Selena guides us to know where we accumulate our highest vibrational energy. As someone who works with Black Moon Lilith, I am thrilled to discover more about the powerful White Moon Selena. It is with the embrace of both our Light and our Darkness, the wholeness of our Being, that we step powerfully into Embodied Spirituality."

~ Sandra Bargman, Host of The Edge of Everyday podcast, Author, Luminary Leader, Sacred Stages, LLc
www.SandraBargman.com

"When David first shared with me he was writing a book about the lesser known White Moon, I knew it would be thoroughly researched and truly magical.

I invite you to dive into this work of Goddess Astrology and discover the mysteries and Mythology of Selene within your own birth chart."

~ **Maria Jones, Star Priestess, Stellar Mystery School**
  www.stellarmysteryschool.com

Contents

"I am Selena. I am the illuminator of your soul. I shine from a moon that is not a moon. My light comes from beyond the Gate of Eternity, a portal orbiting your Earth. I am Daughter Moon of the World of Spirit. Call it Avalon. Call it the Elysian Fields. Call it Nirvana. Call it Heaven.

I Illuminate the divine in your soul. I show you your highest aspirations; the version of you that you must ever strive to become. And you will learn that true enlightenment comes not from that which you can never grasp, but from how you strive to reach it."

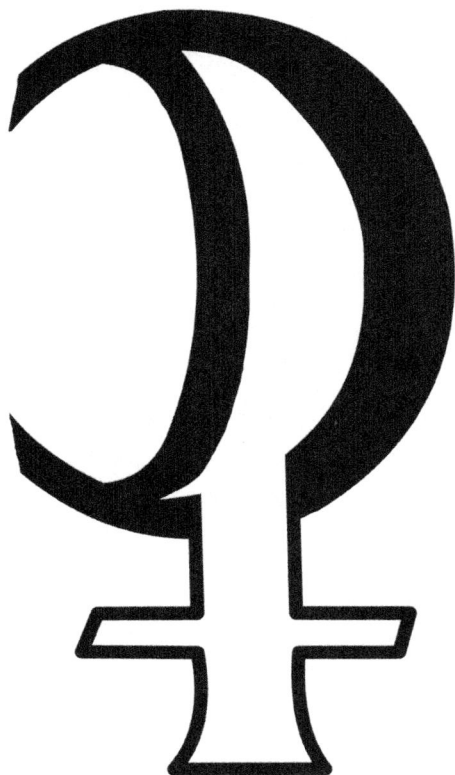

ᑕntroduction

In 2009, in a ceremony on Glastonbury Tor, I dedicated as a Priest of the Goddess. This was at the end of my second year of a three year Priest of Avalon training from the Glastonbury Goddess Temple. That Summer weekend, I chose the symbol I would proudly wear to show the world my calling; my version of a vicar's white collar, if you like. It was a pendant around my neck of a Goddess holding a crescent moon cloak that I bought on Glastonbury High Street in a shop called, ironically (for reasons which will become apparent in the next section), 'Lilith'!

I have worn that pendant visibly every day since then. Whenever I am asked about it (and I am asked often; usually by the person behind the counter in shops) I instantly say "She's my Moon Goddess. She's called Selene." The first time I was asked, the name just came to me instantly. Of course I'd heard of the Goddess Selene over the years, but I have no idea why I should have instinctively picked Her name, particularly, as the Goddess I would now be visibly associated with. Especially since my studies had been almost exclusively devoted to Goddesses of the British Isles.

In 2022 I attended a retreat weekend at the Goddess House in Glastonbury which included a workshop by astrologer and Star Priestess, Kyah May. The natal charts she produced for us included an element I had never heard of before: White Moon Selena. She explained how it represented my highest self and this stuck with me as it was in Taurus, which is (a) ruled by Venus, the Planet of love; and (b) my then-recently deceased wife's Sun Sign.

So the Goddess around my neck, Selene, became not only a symbol of my faith and calling, but also somehow resonant with my two decades plus of an extremely happy and loving marriage. I make it a habit to not ignore signs like that!

I began to include White Moon Selena in my own readings and teachings but I knew I needed to learn more. I looked for books on the subject but there didn't seem to be any. There were a few astrology websites that included it, and very usefully had calculators to work out its position in birth charts. But they were all quite vague and often contradictory as to what White Moon Selena actually is.

Consulting my astrology teacher and mentor, Maria Jones gave me the answer I needed... certainly not the one I was expecting... but needed. She told me that if there isn't a book about it then I would have to write it myself!

Well, I am no stranger to the publishing world. I was, at varying times, designer, editor and publisher of *Pagan Dawn* magazine for nearly a decade and had even penned the occasional article too in that time. And thankfully VisionWeaver Press is providing the regular kicks I need to get the words out of my head and into my keyboard at a decent rate (because my Saturn is in the Ninth House and so my self-discipline is firmly focused on what I want to do *next* or on anything other than what I am supposed to be doing *now!*)

To tune into the energies of White Moon Selena in each Sign, to properly intuit and interpret its effects and energies as they relate to the mythology of the Goddess Selene, I am writing the bulk of this book over the course of a lunar month, starting of course at a New Moon. Every two or three days, the moon moves through each of the twelve Signs and I am writing about each Sign and ruling Planet during the time the Moon is in that Sign.

1. What, and Where, is "White Moon Selena"?

This is a very difficult question to answer. If you try to research the definition of White Moon Selena online the authors of various websites will talk about it as the opposition point to the better-known Black Moon Lilith. They state that if Lilith is the point of apogee of the Moon's orbit, i.e. the point at which the Moon is furthest away from Earth, then Selena would be the *perigee*, the closest point to Earth of the Moon's orbit.

If that were to be the case, then logically, in an elliptical orbit, Selena would have the same nine year rotation as Lilith and always be in the opposite Sign/House (give or take a few degrees to account for irregularities in the orbit).

But that just isn't the case. The few websites out there that offer White Moon Selena produce results that are way off that definition. My own, for example, puts Lilith and Selena *in conjunction*. This was something I could not get my head around until I started digging deeper.

Going down the rabbit hole of successive links on the internet, I eventually reached the "Swiss Ephemeris", a computer ephemeris for developers of astrological software, produced by Astrodeinst. Deep within this document was section 2.7.6, under *'Hypothetical Bodies'*:

"*[Selena/White Moon] is a 'hypothetical' second Moon of the Earth (or a third one, after the "Black Moon") of obscure provenance. Many Russian astrologers use it. Its distance from the Earth is more*

3

than 20 times the distance of the Moon and it moves about the Earth in 7 years. Its orbit is a perfect, unperturbed circle. Of course, the physical existence of such a body is not possible. The gravities of Sun, Earth, and Moon would strongly influence its orbit."

The fact that it has a perfect circular orbit is proof that it cannot exist on this physical plane. Johannes Kepler established in his first two Laws of Planetary Motion in 1609 that a planet's orbit has to be irregular and elliptical.

Some astrologers try to separate out the confused multiple definitions and give different names and astrological qualities given to the actual Moon perigee: 'Light Moon Arta' is one, 'Priapus' is another. Astrologer Richard Nolle, even suggested 'Eve' as the logical opposition to 'Lilith'! It does not stop many astrological websites from continually defining White Moon Selena as the Lunar Perigee while offering natal chart placements based on the hypothetical second moon (positioned as 'h56' on Astrodeinst).

The concept of White Moon Selena has its origins in the work of Pavel Pavlovich Globa (1953-), possibly one of the most famous and influential astrologers in Russia and the founder of the Avestan School of Astrology.

According to *The Avesta*, the sacred book of Zoroastrianism, the work upon which Globa based his astrological principles, the universe is divided into two worlds: the physical, natural world we can see and touch and the invisible, spiritual world of the gods. The process of life in the universe is composed of a struggle between light and darkness. When one of these two forces defeats the other in the material realm then time will end and the physical world will merge with the spiritual world.

Globa wrote "According to ancient Avesta teaching, the Planets were originally cosmic bodies projecting onto the Earth God's grace, poured out throughout the cosmos. Evil, having burst into our system, distorted this projection, introduced a devilish principle into it. From that moment on, the Planets by their nature became dual for us. Now they carry both angelic and devilish origins."

Certainly this principle (if you leave aside such pejorative terms as 'angelic' and 'devilish') is well recognised in astrology in the form of the 'shadow' sides of ourselves being negatively impacted by energies of the Signs and Planets.

In accordance with the second principle of Zoroastrianism, that people have free will and free choice, Globa (2001) suggested that everyone has good and evil within them and that astrology provides a map, directing a person in what they have to work on and what they have to change in themselves. That is, how to inform a choice to move towards and enhance their "good" and move away from their "evil". He said, "The main goal should not be prediction, but the modelling of the desired version of events, as well as the prevention of the undesirable variant."

This principle is an interpretation of how we balance a negative astrological effect on our shadows within one Zodiac Sign by invoking and following the light and positive messages within the opposite Sign; fight a shadow Aquarius effect by bringing in a positive light quality of Leo, for example.

One of the astrological powers that has been long understood to represent our darker sides is Black Moon Lilith, which is the point of apogee of the Moon's orbit around the Earth. According to Costa Rican astrologer, Juan Antonio Revilla, it "seems to have been introduced into astrological practice in France by Don Neroman (Pierre Rougié, 1884–1953) in the early or mid-1930s. He apparently was also the first to call it 'Black Moon'." It may be our 'dark' side or simply an uncomfortable part of ourselves which we prefer to keep hidden. Either way, it represents a truth deep within us that defines our present state.

Two other points that we need to also consider here are the Lunar Nodes, first written about by Ptolemy, around the 2nd century CE, which signify our pasts and futures (either karmic or ancestral, depending on one's beliefs).

Revilla wrote, "they all represent idealized focal points or "directions" that are a result of the "psychic projections" of the Moon, they are "**Moon ghosts**" that the Moon always carries with it, that are part of the "lunar structure" of every individual. The Moon represents the present moment, the nodes, apsides, and empty focus represent the past and "look forward" psychic projections that give shape and structure to the lunar dynamics of a person's life. They are like the rooms, passages and corridors of a house (the different parts of the orbit) that become projections of the person who inhabits it (the Moon)."

This triad of Descending Node, Black Moon Lilith and Ascending Node fit very neatly with the Avestan view. It becomes the past, present and future, described in Zurvanite texts (an extinct branch of Zoroastrianism) as the "three finite times". The three times are combined into "the point of eternity". It is this single point that Globa identified as White Moon Selena; a natural reaction, in the Avestan view, to the existence of Black Moon Lilith, being the 'good, light' counterpart to the 'evil, dark' Lilith.

But if White Moon Selena (which Globa originally named 'Isis' in his first writing on the subject) was simply the opposite of Black Moon Lilith, then it might as well have been positioned at the lunar perigee. But the addition of the Nodes to the idea turned a simple opposition into a cross, which was a symbol of the Vara, a paradise or island of the blessed in Zoroastrian myth.

Russian astrologer Albert Timashev described the four points, or corners of Vara, as the "Gates of Eternity", the way through to Akarana, the "point of the undivided time" in the Zurvanist texts.

However, Timashev was not satisfied with Globa's "stormy fantasy" of White Moon Selena and set out to find an astronomical formula to replace the empirical ephemerides that arose in the initial years of the Avesta School between 1985–1988. He used the Solar Apogee, the point of the Earth's orbit which is the greatest distance from the Sun, a nearly fixed point at around 13 degrees Cancer, as a basis to work out a calculation for what he called "True Light Moon Arta". Working with contemporary, Alexander Smirnov, Timashev found a calculation for the "Light Moon" that used the positions of True Black Moon Lilith, the True Node and the Solar Apogee and came up with a position that had an orbit of 6 years, 11 months and 10 days, i.e. 6.95 years.

It is very close, but it does still not quite add up to the perfect seven years that was originally intuited by Globa. Thus Timashev's 'Light Moon Arta' has to remain a valid, but separate and distinct astrological entity.

So if we accept White Moon Selena as a "point of eternity" or a way to Akarana, then it follows that the point is a portal to a divine power in the spiritual realms; a power that brings illumination to our own highest divine selves. Seen this way, White Moon Selena stops being a 'hypothetical' or 'imaginary' moon and starts to become a *mythical* one.

We can envisage this mythical moon's illuminating power as the Goddess Selene Herself; shining over a spiritual realm and through the portal to us. You can call this spiritual realm Akarana, the Elysian Fields, Avalon, Valhalla, Nirvana or simply Heaven. She is Heaven's Moon. We cannot visually see Her in our physical night sky, but Her effect is there and is felt by us just the same.

2. What is the Astrological Nature of White Moon Selena?

So why would we work with a planetary body that doesn't exist in our reality and doesn't even have the virtue of being an actual astronomical point, like Black Moon Lilith, True Arta and the Lunar Nodes? Why should a hypothetical, even 'mythical', point have an astrological quality?

More than any other infinite number of locations in the night that a hypothetical moon *could* be located, White Moon Selena has the virtue of being a perfect point. Its seven year orbit is an aspect of its perfection.

In the Bible the 7th Day was made holy after the six days of creation. There are seven deadly sins and seven sacraments in the Catholic Church. The Book of Revelations includes references to seven trumpets, seven seals, seven angels, seven churches, and seven plagues. The sacred geometric symbol, *The Seed of Life* consists of seven circles.

In the *Rigveda*, the earliest book of the Hindu Vedas, there are seven heavenly fortresses, seven rays of the sun, seven seasons, seven Adityas (benevolent gods), seven races of men, and seven parts of the world.

Buddha teaches of seven steps to enlightenment and, when newborn, took seven steps.

There are the seven major chakra points in the body. There are seven musical notes in an octave. And there were seven Planets in classical astrology. So there is a lot of history for seven to be a perfect spiritual number.

So White Moon Selena is both perfect and non-existent. That seeming-dichotomy is the root of White Moon Selena's power and qualities.

Imagine a mountain on a shoreline. There might be an infinite number of places to stand but only one spot on this whole mountain that offers the perfect view of the perfect sunset. Seeking White Moon Selena is spending a lifetime walking around the mountain trying to find that perfect vantage point.

Therefore the White Moon Selena point has the quality of aspiring to perfection, which works alongside modern astrology's common definition of White Moon Selena as being the 'highest aspiration'. But crucially, this point of perfection might never be found or might not even be possible for us to achieve. A lifetime of aspiration towards perfection, and constant failure to achieve it. In the chapters that follow, I call this 'The White Shadow'.

Depressed yet?

Well, if you are an Earth Sign, like Capricorn, then this unrealised ambition may well get you down. But a Pisces might well enjoy living in the fantasy world of this aspiration and never worry about making it real.

Although Zurvanite Astrology, where the concepts behind White Moon Selena originate, tended towards the fatalistic ("it is not possible to strive against fate. For once a thing is fated and comes true, whether for good or the reverse" *Mēnōg-ī Khrad, 'Spirit of Wisdom',* circa 6th century), there are well established techniques for compensating for adverse portents in the Planets and Signs.

The divine power of White Moon Selena means that it exalts (i.e. has its greatest power) in whatever Sign it happens to be in. Which means that it has a corresponding 'fall', the place that drains its impact, in the opposing Sign. So if you are feeling the White Shadow of White Moon Selena's demands in Capricorn, you can compensate by invoking 'A Hint of Shade' and follow the guidance of the Planets in Cancer.

And whatever your Sign, seeking the highest aspiration of White Moon Selena might lead you to somewhere on the way – and that's further than you'd get if didn't have the aspiration.

After all, as Mick Jagger said, "You can't always get what you want. But if you try some time, you might just find, you get what you need!"

3. Selene - A Goddess' Story

"She's there behind the glass, a different universe just millimetres from his fingertips, with everything she represents. Divine light."

— Alan Moore, *Unearthing*

In this chapter I will endeavour to summarise the *Her*story of Selene, the Greek Goddess of the Moon. In the astrological chapters to follow, I will be using elements of Selene's mythology in my divination of how White Moon Selena finds expression in each of the Signs and Planets. Here is where these disparate elements can be seen in context.

Before I begin, however, I must pay tribute to the writer, Steve Moore (1949–2014). Moore worked primarily as a UK comics writer in the 1970s and early 1980s, where I first encountered his works. He was also an editor of *Fortean Times* and *Fortean Studies*.

He was, as he put it himself in a 2011 interview, "born at the full moon atop a crescent shaped hill, the main mineral being Selenite."

After receiving the word "Endymion" in a dream, leading him to the John Keats poem of the same name, Moore eventually, in 1989, paints the image of a woman against the Moon in a turquoise night; a woman that had been prophesied to him by a palm reader in 1976. This image sits on his bedroom wall from then on as his inspiration (referenced in the Alan Moore quote above).

Following his explorations of Endymion, which included journeying to Mount Latmos, he began an extensive research project. Moore sought to extract the original mythology of Selene from out of the modern Robert Graves and Women's Mysteries neo-Pagan reimaginings of Her power and mythology. This was not to deny Her modern relevance and interpretations, but to identify and explore the original Greek and Cretan sources.

He used much of his research in his 2011 novel, *Somnium: A Fantastic Romance* a partially self-referential story about a writer trying to compose a book about Selene and Her romantic encounters in dream with an Elizabethan author 'Endimion Lee'.

Moore died on 16th March 2014, a mere two days after completing his final edits on the manuscript of *Selene: The Moon Goddess and Cave Oracle;* his comprehensive academic researches into Selene's mythology. The book was eventually published in 2019 and was returned as a print-on-demand paperback in 2023. In my opinion, Steve Moore's researches are the definitive work on the original, Classical Era mythology of Selene. I recommend that anyone who wishes to go beyond the summary of Selene's mythology in this chapter should seek out this book.

Selene's parents were of the Titans who preceded the pantheon of the Olympian Gods. Her father was Hyperion ('The One Above') and Her mother was Theia (simply 'The Goddess'). Selene had a brother, Helios ('The Sun') and a sister Eos ('The Dawn'). Hyperion and Theia were brother and sister, but that was hardly uncommon in ancient mythologies. The relationships and family ties of Gods and Goddesses tended to shift with successive retelling of the stories and, in any case, parenting does not usually follow the same rules and patterns in mythological 'reality'.

Other accounts name Selene's mother as Aethra or Euryphaëssa ('far shining'), and Her father as Pallas. Sometimes Helios is moved up a generation to be Selene's father instead of brother.

There is also a 1st Century BCE account, by historian Diodorus Siculus of Selene being originally of an Atlantean family who were deified after death and She and Her brother, Helios became the Moon and the Sun respectively.

As babies, Selene and Helios were fostered by the sea-Goddess Tethys, the wife of Ocean. As a baby, Selene gained the mark of a crescent horn on Her forehead.

As Selene grew to womanhood, with Her dark hair and silvery white skin, She was described as second only to Venus in Her beauty. She took on the role and duties of the Moon. Preparing for the ritual of Her nightly duties, She would bathe in the waters of Ocean, with her golden crown lighting up the sky heralding Her imminent appearance. She would don her long, gleaming gown and rise out of the waters at the edge of the World, driving Her chariot. In descriptions and iconography, Her chariot is usually pulled by horses, but later in Her stories, they are bulls. Sometimes they are winged and in one account, Selene is also described as being winged.

Selene is sometimes shown being accompanied in Her nightly ride across the sky by Hermes, in His role as a god of sleep and dreams. Another god of sleep, Hypnos was Her Charioteer.

She never married, but She did have many lovers. Once, after bathing in the waters of Ocean before driving Her chariot across the night sky, She met with Zeus. He left Her pregnant with a beautiful daughter, Pandia (who may have been the inspiration for the ancient Athenian Spring festival of the same name).

Another 'Visible Goddess', Ersa, the personification of dew, is also named as a daughter of Selene and Zeus. With Her brother

Helios, Selene birthed the Goddesses of the Seasons (the Horae): Thallo, Auxo, and Carpo, the personifications of the three seasons recognised by the Greeks, Spring, Summer and Autumn.

The mystical poets, Musaeus and Epimenides are noted as sons of Selene; the former by Orpheus, the musician who travelled with the Argonauts, and the latter by Eumolpus, the founder of the Eleusinian Mysteries.

The infamous Narcissus, who was so handsome he fell in love with his own reflection, was said to have been the offspring of Selene and Endymion, and another similarly beautiful boy, Ampelos was said to have the same heavenly beauty of his mother, Selene.

The horned and goat-legged Pan was not a lover of Selene, but He did trick Her into laying with Him by surrounding Himself with a snowy fleece in order to appear beautiful to Her. This act was considered quite scandalous by the Latin writers of the time, indicating that the Greek Selene was beginning to evolve into aspects of the Roman Diana, who was considered virginal.

By far the most famous of Selene's lovers was Endymion. In fact, this story was so famous that all accounts of it have been lost! Surviving fragments of writing about Selene and Endymion only refer to the story in passing, as if it were so well known, there was no need to repeat it.

So by these fragmented and often contradictory pieces of record, we understand that Endymion was cast into an eternal sleep and Selene fell in love with him, descending every night to make love to him in his cave while he slept. A wall painting in Pompeii shows Endymion reclining in the grip of Hypnos as Selene descended towards him.

The nature of, and reason for Endymion's sleep is vague across the mythology. He was the ruler of Elis, the grandson of Zeus and the founder of the foot-race at the Olympic Games. Or he was a shepherd on Mount Latmos in Caria (South-Western Turkey). He was taken up to heaven by his grandfather, Zeus, whereupon he committed the ultimate faux-pas and fell in love with Zeus' wife Hera. Zeus found out and Endymion begged Zeus to be allowed to sleep forever.

According to a conversation She had with Aphrodite, while driving Her chariot across the night, Selene would often pause when She saw Endymion sleeping out of doors with his 'javelin' in his hand and would go down to be with him. And during these times, the sky would be dark and moonless.

As well as the occasional son, such as Narcissus, Selene had fifty daughters with Endymion. This is a significant number for a man who was connected to the mythology of the Olympics as there are fifty lunar cycles in the four years between the Games.

In between Her lunar duties and visiting Endymion, Selene had other tasks to accomplish. One was a favour to Hera in Her revenge plot against Heracles. Selene magically created the seemingly indestructible Nemean Lion using a large chest filled with foam and froth. The lion, sprung from the chest, was then sent up against Hercules in the first of his legendary Twelve Labours.

Selene apparently also worked in Her spare time as a dream oracle. The Roman author Cicero wrote of a shrine at Thalamae (which is now identified as the village of Koutiphari, 25 miles from Sparta), dedicated to Pasiphae, which was said to be the title of the Moon, and Helios. Spartan rulers would come to the shrine and sleep in order to receive oracle messages from the Goddess in their dreams.

As time moved on and the Greek mythology became subsumed by the Roman, Selene's love for Endymion became progressively more chaste, with the Roman author Cicero telling of Selene giving Endymion nothing more salacious than a chastely kiss as he slept.

During this evolution towards Roman influence, the God Apollo began to take on more and more of Helios' role as the Sun.

And in these patriarchal times, Selene was forcibly transformed into Artemis purely for the reason that Artemis was Apollo's sister, just as Selene was the sister of Helios. Prior to this merging, the virgin huntress Artemis had no association with the Moon in story or iconography. Eventually, Artemis became the fully Roman Diana, and thus Diana took on an association with the Moon.

The Latin author, Servius from the later Roman era, around the 4th Century CE, began to cite the "Triple-Faced Diana" represented by Selene or Luna in the celestial realm, Artemis/Diana in the terrestrial and Prosperina/Persephone in the Underworld. And Selene/Luna Herself is split according to Her phases; birth Goddess Lucina, Huntress Diana and Underworld's Hecate. This is not the same form of 'Triple Moon Goddess' as modern neo-paganism, as put forward by Robert Graves: Maiden, Mother, Crone. There is no evidence of that particular form of Moon Goddess iconography in the Classical period. We can see, however, that there can be seen a through line of evolution of the Moon Goddess to the present.

Selene evolved from being the actual physical Moon to a more spiritual Moon, as described by Servius, in the so-called 'Celestial Sphere'. This evolution is the pin that links, in my view, the mythology of Selene to the power of White Moon Selena. The Celestial Sphere that She moved into is, I believe, located in the Divine Spiritual realms.

She becomes the Moon that shines over the spiritual realms with Her light shining through the 'Gates of Eternity' to that astronomical point (the 'hypothetical' Moon described by Pavel Globa) beyond our physical Moon, circling in Her perfect seven year orbit.

4. How to Use This Book

The first thing you will need to do is get a copy of your birth chart, sometimes also called your natal chart. Many astrological websites offer this, but not many of them include White Moon Selena in the calculations.

On my own website, www.heavensmoon.co.uk, there is a basic chart calculator which will show you your White Moon Selena placement along with the major Planetary aspects.

Then, take note of the Sign, the House and the major Planets aspecting your White Moon Selena. For those unsure, I have included in the relevant chapters a brief description of what aspects and Houses are, and what general effects they have but I recommend other general astrology texts for more detailed explanations about how Houses and aspects work (Steven Forrest's *The Inner Sky* is my favourite).

With that information at hand, the first place to look up in this book is your White Moon Selena House in Chapter 5. I know it seems more natural for most people to want to look up the information about the Sign initially, but I find it more useful to look at the House first.

This is because the twelve Houses define the precise area of our lives that our White Moon Selena's highest aspirations will target. Which side of your life is your divine self-pulling you towards? In the 10th House, it might be related to your career; in the 4th it may point to your home and environment; and so on.

By looking up your House first, you will be able to identify which part of your life we will be looking at, before we go on to look at what effect White Moon Selena will have and how you will be able to work with it.

From there, you can go straight to looking up White Moon Selena's Sign in Chapter 6 which will show how you set about striving for, or expressing your highest aspirations.

For example, we will see how someone with White Moon Selena in Aries will see their highest aspirations as a challenge; a race to be won. In Cancer, one would seek to attain their divine self by being everything to everyone.

As I said in Chapter 2, striving for our highest aspirations may be very fruitful in itself but with the best will in the world, there's no guarantee we can ever fully achieve them. So along with each Sign, we will also look at what I call 'The White Shadow' which is the adverse impact of White Moon Selena's Sign; how striving to achieve your highest aspirations can affect you in a challenging way and throw you off track. Then tinting your 'White' with 'A Hint of Shade' suggests invoking Astrological strategies for coping with the Shadow.

If the Sign and House are the main ingredients of this astrological meal, we then come to the seasoning. No Planetary body in our chart acts in isolation. The location of the other Planets can add a bit of seasoning and extra flavour to the meal; sometimes sweet, sometimes spicy!

In the section on Planets, in Chapter 7, see what effect the other bodies in the sky are having on your White Moon Selena placement.

As an aside, in strict astronomical terms, the Sun and Moon are obviously not planets like Mars or Venus, say. And Pluto drifts in and out of classification as a planet every few years. But in astrology, all the bodies that move across our sky: Sun, Moon, regular planets, dwarf planets, asteroids, hypothetical objects and, of course our spiritual White Moon Selena, are all called 'Planets' in terms of their astrological effects.

Look at where the other Planets are in your birth chart and see the basic underlying effects of their placements. Then look at a present day chart and take note of how today's Planets are aligned with your natal White Moon Selena placement (or how today's White Moon Selena placement is aligning with the natal placement of your other Planets). These are called 'transits' and will show a current, temporary effect on your evolution towards your divine self.

You can read and enjoy this book without knowing your birth chart details. The mythology of Goddess Selene and the development of astrological White Moon Selena are fascinating stories in themselves, for one thing.

However there is also much to be said about how we deal with our own personal quests for perfection and high aspirations. You certainly don't need to have a specific White Moon Selena placement to experience the urge to continually improve something until it reaches some distant goal of perfection (which now makes me wonder where George Lucas' White Moon Selena is, considering how many changes he made to *Star Wars* over the years!). I like to think we can use astrological themes and archetypes, such as those in this book, to help us cope with our occasional drives towards over-perfectionism in any area of life.

If you do know your birth chart, though, you will be able to target the precise influences White Moon Selena is having on your life. If you do not know your precise birth time, putting in an approximate time within an hour will usually work to identify your House layout, as long as White Moon Selena is not too close to a House boundary (called a 'cusp'). If you have no idea of your birth time, just choose 6am. You may not be able to accurately identify the House placements but the positions of White Moon Selena and the other Planets within the Signs will still be accurate and give you a lot of information to work with.

After you have worked through this book, if you want to take things further and get a personal detailed analysis of your White Moon Selena and its impact on your life and highest aspirations, you can get in touch with me through my website and I would be happy to book a full consultation with you.

In a personal session we work through your whole birth chart, looking at not just your White Moon Selena impact but how your other Planetary placements work for you. We will also look at your present and future placements to understand how the focus of your highest aspirations shift over time. And don't worry, I have a technique to identify your House placements if you do not know your precise birth time.

See Chapter 10 at the end of the book for more details.

But for now, go and look up your birth chart and with all that in hand, let's begin with the Houses...

5. The Twelve Houses of White Moon Selena

The Houses are the twelve divisions of the day. The first six, below the horizon relate to our inner needs and the second six, above the horizon relate to our place in the outer world. The Sign and Planets on the Eastern horizon at our time of birth are contained in our First House and define our Ascendent. The rest of the Houses work their way down and around the sky from there.

Each House is related to our roles in the World; a slice of life. White Moon Selena's placement in your House chart will describe which part of your life will your highest aspirations be directed towards. Will it be on your status in society? Your love life? Changing the world?

The Houses are associated with the twelve Signs and their ruling Planets so you can intuit more about the nature of each House by looking at the chapters in this book on their associated Signs and Planets.

As ever, with White Moon Selena, your reach for the ideal will usually be beyond your grasp. So you need to be mindful of tempering your expectations by giving some focus to the energies of the opposing Signs. The suggestions I give will hopefully help you take a pause in your aspirations and enjoy the benefits of where you are rather than always on the future.

First House – The House of Personality

Associated with Aries and Mars, it also includes the Ascendant. This is the House which defines the face with which we show the world. With White Moon Selena in this House, your highest aspirations are somewhere in the field of self-development. Your inner divine self needs to be pulled to the surface and projected for the world to see. This is not, however, a false glamour of mere self-confidence. If it takes education, therapy or physical fitness training to 'be all you can be' then so be it.

If you want to conquer (as an Arian would put it) this self-obsession, you may wish to invoke the tactics of Libra and balance your own self-image by looking for a second point of view. Listen to your colleagues, friends or partner and see what they see in you rather than how you see yourself.

Second House – The House of Money

Associated with Taurus and Venus, this is more appropriately considered as the House of self-esteem and self-worth. With White Moon Selena placed in the Second House the challenge arises as to how far you are willing and able to go to prove yourself to yourself? Are you a collector who is always hunting for 'just one more' to complete a set (a set that will never be really complete because there's always 'just one more'!) Are you always searching for an elusive 'perfect partner' in your love life? Are you constantly chasing promotion after promotion at work?

Invoke the Scorpion to stop focusing on future perfection and concentrate on, as Eckhart Toll put it, 'the power of now'. Try some mindfulness exercises to see the beauty in what you already are and what you have. How would you set about enjoying the day if you knew it was to be your last?

Third House – The House of Communication

Associated with Gemini and Mercury, this is the domain of taking in and sharing information in all its forms. Knowledge for the pure sake of knowing. In the days of Leonardo da Vinci, there was the concept of 'the Renaissance Man', which was defined as someone who studies a wide variety of fields. And in the limited world of the 15th century, it might even have been possible to learn *everything*. Read every book and master every skill known. Even if it was possible then, it certainly isn't now. But the 'eternal student' with White Moon Selina in the Third House will certainly give it a fair attempt.

Stop taking endless courses. There's a time to stop learning and start doing. Invoke the Sagittarian drive for innovation and try using your skills and knowledge to create something. Write a book instead of just reading them, for example. Look for a new job that makes use of your lifelong learning. Or *invent* a new job.

Fourth House – The House of the Home

Associated with Cancer and the Moon, the Fourth House is in the position of midnight on the Star Wheel. The perfect time for the Moon. It is also the place where you need the ultimate protection. With White Moon Selena in the Fourth House you may feel a need to build the perfect shell to hide from the world. Priority becomes security. in Taurus, this might be a comfortable safe home. In Sagittarius, on the other hand, safety might be found in running away when the pressures of others become too strong. Either way, your highest aspiration is to be isolated behind your shell from the overbearing influences of the outside world so you can swim freely in your own sensitive depths.

The perfect home generally comes at a cost. There's going to be a mortgage or rent to pay. The Capricorn sea-goat can swim you out of your cosy depths and tell you to pay the bills. By taking this responsibility for your own needs, if you want to build a better shell, you have to learn to come *out* of it first.

Fifth House – The House of Children

Associated with Leo and the Sun, the Fifth House is where we like to play; where we can let our inner child run free, indulging in the full creative expression of our talents and interests, purely for the pleasure of it. With White Moon Selena in the Fifth House, our highest aspiration will likely be something that brings joy and happiness in your life. It doesn't matter whether you are happy being the life and soul of the party or focused on your career goals or sitting for hours in silent meditation. As long as you are doing it primarily for pleasure and happiness.

But if life is feeling a bit shallow in your hedonistic pursuit of pleasure, you can compensate by getting serious and invoking Aquarian revolutionary spirit. Why not get involved in a campaign for rights and freedoms in society, whether it be animal rights, gender rights, political freedoms, etc? All of which would ultimately have the effect of making more people happy anyway.

Sixth House – The House of Service

Associated with Virgo and Mercury, the Sixth House is where we are of service. It can be to a loved one, to a family or community or to the world. The latter, service to the world is the expression of White

Moon Selena in the Sixth House. Your highest aspiration is to be of the greatest service to the greatest number of people. You employ your talents, in whatever form you are most suited, for the good of the many. In Aquarius, you may desire to change the system. In Gemini, your words propel you to be an influential teacher. In Pisces, you may feel the call to priesthood. The means and the method is immaterial. Whatever your role in life, your motives, deep down, are pure; working to an end that will make the world a better place. Even just a little bit.

Endless altruism, though, can be wearying. No matter how personally satisfying, there will always be a part of you craving a bit of service for yourself. A bit of time out for some Piscean inward looking self-care for your soul would not go amiss. Try some meditation, yoga, sound baths or even go backpacking off to 'find yourself'. Let the rest of the world look after itself for a bit.

Seventh House – The House of Marriage

Associated with Libra and Venus, the Seventh House is where we form partnerships. It is usually thought of as romantic partnerships but it can also be a creative or business partner. Or even that best mate who always shows up and knows exactly how to cheer you up when you are down. There's a little moment of magic when you meet that special someone that you can identify with and who seems to be your soul reflection. With White Moon Selena in your Seventh House, you tend to feel like you are half a soul, constantly looking for the other half to be complete. Your ideal partner is someone who is likely to be a complete mirror image of yourself, so you can end up being one of those irritating couples who finish each other's sentences.

To temper this long and possibly fruitless quest, try and follow the Aries pattern of boldly striking out on your own. Take the occasional solo holiday in a far off land, spending time with people very different from you, where you may even conquer the heart of someone completely unsuitable, who may turn out to be just who you need.

Eighth House – The House of Death

Associated with Scorpio and Pluto, this is the House where we consider our legacy. How do we live beyond our deaths? In this House we have our sex lives; the mating urge; the need to have children that carry our genes forward. Or it can be the need to do or create something that makes us be remembered long after we are gone. White Moon Selena in this House is literally our Immortal Souls. Our highest aspirations are to 'live forever'. It is a drive to achieve something that will make us remembered throughout history. But will we be an Abraham Lincoln or a John Wilkes Booth?

It is a nice thought to be remembered and, hopefully, honoured. But we can't always worry about the future. Turn your gaze downward and, like a Taurus, appreciate the ground you walk on. A Scorpio has the power to live entirely for the moment, so use it and take some time to enjoy beauty and life as it is. Look at the world through your eyes, not through your camera lens. Posterity can take care of itself.

Ninth House – The House of Long Journeys Over Water

Associated with Sagittarius and Jupiter, this is the House of personal development. In this House, the Planets define how we can progress in our lives, avoiding stagnation as we change our outlooks on life through new experiences. It could be a physical journey to far off lands or an inner voyage of discovery through meditation. White Moon Selena in this House is apt to make us very restless and unable to settle in one home or career or with one lover. There is apt to be a constant need to move on, meeting new people in new exciting places.

It is difficult to overcome this desire to always move forward but invoking Gemini is a way to do it without forever abandoning your loved ones. Sometimes there's nothing better than a good book to transport you to a far off land. A period of intellectual study can provide an antidote for itchy feet while still providing new insights and experiences to keep the Ninth House in order.

Tenth House – The House of Career

Associated with Capricorn and Saturn, this House is concerned with your place in the world and how you are seen; your career, status and public identity. The entrance to this House is the Midheaven, which is the Sign that was directly overhead in the sky, shining the greatest light at your time of birth. White Moon Selena in this House brings a need for recognition. You want everyone to acknowledge your status and see the value in what your soul feels called to bring to the world. This is not because of pride or ego, but for your effectiveness. The more the world recognises what you offer, the more you will be able to offer it.

So, how do we cope if we don't receive the recognition we need? Like a Cancerian we have to put our own needs behind a shell for a while. If we can't be what we want to be then, like many in an over competitive job market, we have to spend some time being what *someone else* needs us to be. Just for a while. Until we can make this role into our own.

Eleventh House – The House of Friends

Associated with Aquarius and Uranus, this House is concerned with social structures, such as family, clan and friendships. This seems ironic when connected to the Sign and Planet of individuality but it makes sense when we consider that we look for people in our lives who support our unique outlook or even share it; people we can be ourselves with without judgement. White Moon Selena in this House brings a need for collaboration; a desire to surround ourselves with people who can either help us strive towards our highest aspirations, or share the same or similar aspirations.

We may become lost or adrift without such people around us so we must invoke Leo and take to the stage. No hiding your dreams away. Turning a spotlight on ourselves will bring the right people to you.

Twelfth House – The House of Troubles

Associated with Neptune and Pisces, this is the House of great turning points and crisis in our lives. The Planets and Signs placed within this House at our birth define how we respond when the chips are down. White Moon Selena in this House points to your highest aspirations in the realm of enlightenment; seeking to achieve the inner strength to live in a stress-free state of grace whereby no adversity can affect your equilibrium.

If enlightenment is proving elusive, try following a little of Virgo's example and maybe do a little volunteering or charity work. Sometimes a little attention of other people's problems can do wonders in taking your mind off your own.

6. White Moon Selena in the Stars

As the point of White Moon Selena orbits the Earth in its seven year journey, like all the other planetary bodies, it moves across the sky passing in front of the 12 constellations that make up the Zodiac. It takes roughly seven months to move across one Sign and into the next.

It's common for people to say casually, "I'm an Aquarius – I do things my own way" or "I'm an Aries – I like to take charge". But they are really describing which Sign the Sun was moving through at the time they were born, and the influence that the combination of Sun and Sign has on a person: their core identity.

Every Planet has its own effect. Your Moon Sign describes how you respond emotionally; your Venus Sign influences the patterns of your love life; and so on

In the next section we will explore your White Moon Selena Sign: the Zodiac constellation that the White Moon Selena point was moving through at the time you were born. Let us now look at what it means to have White Moon Selena in each one of the 12 Signs...

White Moon Selena in Aries ♈

> *"Whensoever bright Selene, having bathed Her lovely body in the water of ocean, and donned her far-gleaming raiment, drives on her long-maned horses at full speed, at eventide in the mid-month: then her great orbit is full and then Her beams shine brightest as She increases. So She is a sure token and a sign to mortal men. Hail, white-armed Goddess, bright Selene, mild, bright-tressed Queen! Show us Thy Beauty."*
>
> — Olivia Robertson, *Urania, Ceremonial Magic of the Goddess; Lunar Magic of the Tides*

At the beginning of her journey across the night, She is resurrected, like Springtime. Rising out of the Ocean Stream of Pisces-dream, Selene dons Her luminous gowns to shine Her light over the dark Earth.

And so it begins in Aries, the Fire Sign that leads the procession of the Zodiac. In this case, though, with White Moon Selena, the fire is possibly better expressed in its aspect of light or illumination, in Her full-moon form, burning a path through the darkness of night and revealing all that is hidden within. Indeed, Moore explains that the very name, Selene, could be derived from the Greek word *selas*, meaning 'light' or 'brightness', and that She is described as the "white armed Goddess". He suggests "Selene, in putting on her 'shining raiment' is, effectively, dressing herself in Moonlight... it's quite certain that illumination is her main function as a visible Goddess."

Aries is the Sign of pure and true determination and courage. It is the warrior spirit that needs to fight, to overcome challenges. Life is a never ending series of contests with each victory merely being the qualifier for the next round. Nothing stands in the way of an Ariean and their target.

But to reach the target of destiny you have to be able to see it first. This is the power of White Moon Selena in Aries: in Her piercing light, you see the authentic truth of your divine self. You are able to see the route to your highest aspirations with pinpoint clarity, like a beacon in the night... shining with the intensity of the full Moon in a cloudless sky.

In the light of White Moon Selena, you see your highest aspirations clearly in front of you. They goad you and entice you. They are the gold medal at the finish line or the pot of gold at the end of the rainbow.

Seeing yourself as your highest self can be quite daunting and exposes all your vulnerabilities. This vision of you where you could be will invariably lead to making comparisons to where you actually are, in reality. You are the vulnerable green shoot of spring looking ahead at the magnificent bloom of Summer. But courage is only worth anything when you are vulnerable. The power of Aries gives you that daring and courage to gain the confidence to believe in your soul that your target can be reached. It is a prize that you will believe it is possible to win.

The White Shadow

And what happens next? That's where it begins to come a bit unstuck, of course. White Moon Selena in Aries only provides the illumination, not the power. Getting to the finish line requires the additional motivation of supporting Planets in appropriately active

Signs to get you off the starting blocks. What else is in Aries? Where is Mars? If your highest aspirations are creative or involve learning, what's happening in Gemini and where is Mercury?

At the end of the day (or should I say night?) the shining beacon of the White Moon Selena in Aries is akin to the shining neon of a Las Vegas strip. Just because you can see the jackpot doesn't mean you will win it. But like a gambler with a 'system', the Aries courage and fighting spirit will always compel you to take one more spin of the wheel.

Unlike other Signs, Aries will never allow you to turn away from your aspirations or settle for less. In the same way that the Moon is always the brightest light in the night, White Moon Selena will continue to show you your divine self and it is like you are wearing blinkers. You stay focused and are seldom distracted by what you deem more trivial goals, unless they can somehow help you stay in the main game. You are going to always feel compelled to reach, to dare, to battle to 'win' and become the champion of your own divinity.

A Hint of Shade

When that need for victory is overriding all else, you need to take a breath and bring in some harmony; the balance that comes from invoking Libra.

Aries may not let you turn away, but you could put extra targets in your sights. Other powerful goals in your life; where is your Sun, or your Venus? Where are they directing you right now? By taking on these extra targets you will inevitably dilute your focus and intensity and scale you back down to a more relaxed and balanced pace.

♉ White Moon Selena in Taurus

"As he was of surpassing beauty, the Moon fell in love with him, and Zeus allowed him to choose what he would, and he chose to sleep forever, remaining deathless and ageless."

— Apollodorus, The Library.

Taurus is the bull, standing serenely in his field. All is well with the world and he has everything he needs in his little field. It is a warm late-spring day, he has his grass to chew on; he has his lovers. His life is luxury because it is at peace. He has everything he needs. They are real and they are around him, ready for when he needs them.

Imagery of Selene often included allusions to bulls. After an early association with horses, She seems in late antiquity to turn Her favours towards the bull. Moore writes that the 2nd Century Greek writer Ptolemy said that Selene was "exalted in Taurus", meaning that the Moon's power was enhanced by Taurean energies. As such, later descriptions of Selene included Her riding bulls or a bull-drawn chariot, or that She was horned, Herself. It is certainly not unusual for bulls' horns to be suggestive of the crescent moon in paintings or statues of Moon related Goddesses.

White Moon Selena in Taurus is your quest for a comfortable, beautiful life. Money, luxury and love are important to Taurus, but they are the means, not the end. Money will buy you that soft sofa to sink into; luxury is the artwork you surround yourself with to satisfy your need to gaze on beauty; love brings you the soul-mate to satisfy your need for family, companionship, sex and a warm cuddle on a cold night.

The Goddess Selene's own obsession was to Her ideal lover, the shepherd Endymion. It was even to the detriment of Her divine role. It was thought that those nights when the Moon was absent (the Dark Moon Phase) it was because She had gone off for an illicit rendezvous with Her lover!

He was astoundingly beautiful, according to myth. The poet Sappho wrote "that Selene went down to Endymion as he slept on Mount Latmos." And Lucien satirically described how Selene would watch him "sleeping out of doors in hunter's fashion" with his 'javelin' slipping out of his hand.

Unfortunately, Endymion was in no state to enjoy Selena's attentions since, thanks to Zeus, he had to remain asleep.

There are many and varied explanations in ancient writings as to the nature of Endymion's endless sleep, but it does seem that it was something he chose in order to be able to receive the love of Selene. With the obvious consequence being that in order to experience that perfect union, he could *not* experience it. Despite their nocturnal lovemaking producing 50 children, he slept through it all.

It is also relevant to note that Selene was the mother of Narcissus, the man who was so beautiful and, in his obsession with beauty, fell in love with his own reflection. A story emblematic of an obsession with something both beautiful and unattainable.

The White Shadow

With your White Moon Selena in Taurus you are apt to be drawn to the ideal of perfect and harmonious beauty and everything you need to obtain to make it real. And it is never enough. There will always be something that is missing or needs improving on to make it more beautiful. Or for everything you gain, something else gets lost or spoiled.

Like Endymion, you have to pay a steep price in order to achieve the beautiful perfection you seek. Endymion's price, the endless sleep, meant that he was unable to enjoy the beautiful attentions of his shining nocturnal Lover Goddess. (But that seems not to have bothered Selene much, considering She had 50 children with the sleeping Endymion!)

The more you strive to gain more, the less you are able to enjoy it. The family you love dearly still drives you round the bend every so often. The living room isn't quite big enough for all your stuff on display. You can't pass by that craft fair; who knows what beautiful objet d'art might lurk within?

A Hint of Shade

It seems as though nothing but the best will do for the Taurean-White Moon Selena. The challenge is to be able to accept that sometimes what you have is good enough. You may always be tempted to think that you'll be happier if you have more or bigger or better, but take the inspiration of Scorpio and imagine how it would be if today was your final day on this world. Take the time to enjoy the luxuries you already have and all the beauty you have created around you before looking for the next addition to your collection.

White Moon Selena in Gemini ♊

"When the sun set and the Moon appeared I invoke Diana-Selene-Hecate, I offer her my love and ask for her help. And then I write in Bacchic frenzy 'neath the beaming Moon, barely sane, pen a-dancing, words appearing in my fervid brain and scribbled scrawlish all across the page to get them down before they are lost. Because they come from Dreamland."

— Moore, Somnium.

Among the legends of Endymion's great sleep *(See chapter 3 and under Taurus)*, are the stories that he chose to sleep in order to 'know' Selene. And there are two ways to interpret that. One way is discussed under Taurus. The other is to look at Selena's role as a dream oracle.

There were shrines and temples in antiquity dedicated to dream oracles, where people could go and sleep in order to hear messages from oracles and goddesses in their dreams.

Pausanias, in his *Description of Greece* (2nd Century CE) describes a sanctuary with an oracle on the road from Oetylus to Thalamae which contained bronze statues of Pasiphae and Helios, noting that "Pasiphae is a title of the Moon (Selene), and is not a local goddess of the people of Thalamae". Moore notes "Pasiphae derives from *pasi* meaning 'for all' and from *phaino* 'to bring to light, to make clear, to disclose, to give light, to shine forth'." So the title refers to the one who brings light for all. Which certainly applies in the literal sense to The Moon as well as in the oracular context to Selene.

The crucial relevance here is that a visitor goes to sleep in the shrine in a specially prepared 'bridal chamber' and meets the oracle within a dream. The Roman writer, Cicero, in his work *On Divination*, also writes of Spartan rulers sleeping in a shrine of Pasiphae to receive oracles in their dreams.

So was Endymion's motive in 'knowing' Selene literally just that? 'Knowing' in the sense of receiving Selena's illuminating words of wisdom rather than Her more lustful favours? Perhaps. But there's still the 50 children to take into account. It seems that maybe Selene could be considered the Goddess of Pillow Talk!

Gemini is an Air Sign and thus is one of the domains of intellectual pursuits in the Zodiac. Specifically, it is the Sign of knowledge; both receiving it and disseminating it. Geminis make natural journalists and gossips (sometimes one and the same thing). And the highest aspiration of any journalist is the 'scoop'. They aspire to be the first to learn some new exiting piece of information and getting it out to the public before anyone else. A gossip does much the same.

Divination, whether it be by card, palm, crystal ball or tea leaves, is a time honoured method of gleaning hidden information. No matter whether you consider it to be coming from a divine oracle or dragged up from the depths of your subconscious (and some would say there's no substantive difference between the two). Perhaps the most famous and popular divination method is the Tarot. Some divine oracles seem to live within the images on the cards, transmitting their messages 'hardwired' via archetypes into our consciousness.

The Tarot card of the High Priestess denotes a powerful looking woman who is the keeper of sacred knowledge. She sometimes keeps it safely hidden and sometimes reveals it when it is needed. The moon crescent that appears in the usual depictions of the character indicate that she could be interpreted as a Moon Goddess, especially in her messages being sometimes hidden and sometimes revealed, like the phases of The Moon Herself.

The twin pillars of wisdom either side of the High Priestess are reminiscent of the Sign of Gemini itself and one could easily imagine them as Gemini's twin ears, ready to listen and absorb any information that the High Priestess cares to share.

This, then, appears to be the role of White Moon Selena in Gemini. The aspirations of illumination and revelation; to achieve the ultimate 'scoop'. I feel the highest aspiration is to learn something new; to receive or uncover a 'divine revelation' of knowledge that nobody else has ever heard of or thought of before. And when they reveal it, they dream it could change the world as we know it.

Detectives feel the energy of the Gemini-White Moon Selena too (at least those in popular fiction, real life ones may be a little more prosaic). They exhibit an inability to let go of a mystery, like a dog with a bone. The shabby little man in a raincoat on Sunday afternoon TV, tirelessly pursuing every little clue until the web of deceit is unravelled and the light of truth is laid bare for all to see. All it takes is to ask, "just one more thing!"

The White Shadow

I feel it would be easy for the person with White Moon Selena in Gemini to become the eternal student. Listening, learning, discovering new tidbits of information and data; it could never end. Alternately, instead of diving deep down in one field, Gemini's restlessness can turn you into a butterfly, flitting from one topic to another, trying to learn a little of everything; or worse, a *lot* of everything! Whatever your path in life, there is practically no limit to how long you could study to become more and more of an expert without ever actually putting any of that knowledge to any use.

A Hint of Shade

If Geminis are the explorers of the intellectual realm, then Sagittarians are the explorers of the physical world, hunting for dragons on a lost continent. To continue to satisfy the Gemini urge for knowledge while also getting your nose out of a book, you can invoke the Sagittarian spirit of adventure, gaining experience to go alongside knowledge. Travel somewhere and learn by *doing.* If indeed you are cursed with being the eternal student, at the very least try to do an exchange year somewhere.

Ꮤ White Ꮇoon Selena in Cancer 69

*"The best way to find yourself is to lose
yourself in the service of others"*

— Mahatma Gandhi

To live in the water Sign of Cancer is the struggle to sink or swim in the depths of emotion: your own emotions and also your sensitivity to those around you. Of the four classical elements, water has always been the domain of our emotional lives. Cancerians feel motions swirl through and around them so deeply that they need to develop their hard shell of protection, like the crab that symbolises their Sign. And they cover their defensiveness by dealing with other people's issues in order to avoid dealing with their own.

They are the mother archetype; the nurturer who always puts her charges' needs before her own.

Selene loved Endymion with all Her heart and soul but he, being asleep, was incapable of expressing his love back to Her. Denied the experience of feeling the devotion of Her lover, She appears to have retreated behind the Cancer shell of coping by nurturing. Hence becoming the mother of 50 children with him (this is as well as the numerous children She had by other lovers in Her time).

Whether Selene was a good mother in the modern sense is not recorded in surviving mythology. But there's no question of Her being one of the archetypes of the Great Mother Goddess.

Every month She is seen growing until She is fully rounded, ready to bring life to manifestation in Her bright fullness.

But throughout, She continues her 'day jobs', so to speak, of bringing illumination for all, either in luminescence or as a dream oracle (another example of caring for another's needs) and guiding the tides of the oceans (and women?) in their regular rhythms.

The Cancerian is, above all, sympathetic. The Moon is the ruling Planet of Cancer and shines with the Sun's reflected light. Under the influence of the Moon, Cancerians will tend to pick up habits and mannerisms of the people around them. The surface of the water is Cancer's reflective shell, simultaneously hiding what goes on beneath while showing the viewer a reflection, i.e. being what they want you to be.

They are the fluid that fills any vessel they are poured into.

So we begin to see the path to perfection, the highest aspiration of White Moon Selena in Cancer. She can be a devoted wife, be a nurturing mother, hold down a full time job and, behind Her protective shell, cope with the shifting, turbulent depths of Her own emotional wellbeing.

She is, in fact, the embodiment of the infamous 1980s archetype of the woman who 'has it all'!

She is the devoted wife, nurturing mother, pillar of the community, keeper of the spotless home (Cancer is the Sign of the Fourth House, after all!) and probably could whip up a perfect dinner party at a moment's notice when her husband phones to say the boss has invited himself to dinner. And as well as that, the glossy magazines of the time all said she was expected to be able to pursue a full time fulfilling career as well.

Men are not immune to this pull, either. The primal need and expectations to be the provider who puts the food on the table, the warrior who must look after and protect his family, the builder who can decipher self-assembly furniture instructions while unblocking the sink. And alongside that, can still be the sensitive so-called 'New Man' who is not afraid to cry and show his feelings.

Is it a coincidence that these impossible ideals of men and women were popularised in the same 1980s that also saw the effects of White Moon Selena being discovered by Pavel Globa?

The White Shadow

On TV, back in the 1960s, not even Samantha Stephens could satisfy all those needs and expectations without a little nose-twitching witchcraft. It is the Stepford Wife so-called 'ideal' that nobody could live up to, and nobody would really want to live up to, but somehow even the so-enlightened society of the 21st century still seems to expect in many ways. So what is the result when this Water Sign succeeds in being all things to all people; to be able to put all their own needs aside to be whatever everyone else wants you to be? They get called a 'drip'!

A Hint of Shade

It is time to get real and come down to Earth. When you are overwhelmed by people from all sides expecting your full support, you have to invoke some Capricorn energy and give some support and help to the one person who needs it most: you! You need to spend some time alone doing something that only benefits you. You might not know what that is yet, but being in your own space is the surest way to find out. And if you feel a twinge of guilt that you might be letting everyone else down, then think of it as helping and nurturing them by teaching them how to do without you for a few days.

White Moon Selena in Leo ♌

"For I am sprung from the fair tressed Moon, who in a fearful shudder shook off the savage lion in Nemea, and brought him forth at the bidding of Queen Hera"

— poem fragment by Epimenides (7th century BCE)

The King of the Beasts is ready to roar. Leo is the Sign of self-expression. Everything that would stay hidden beneath the shell of Cancer must find release in Leo.

The Leo personality likes to take centre stage and show the world who they are. They have the gift of 'star quality' with a flamboyant flair for the dramatic.

When your White Moon Selena is in Leo, She brings a sense of freedom to release the inner self. You are not a person who is able to hide who you are. You might be proud of your true self or you might be ashamed of it, but you certainly can't hide it. Your divine self is just you as you really are. I might have said that it is 'you as you really are deep down' but I don't think people with White Moon Selena in Leo really have much of a 'deep down'. They are a fully awake true consciousness from the core, right up to the surface.

In mythology, the Goddess Selene gave birth to a lion. Sometimes the story is that Selene was the literal mother. However, in Demodocus' *History of Heracles*, he describes how Zeus' wife, Queen Hera asked for Selene's help in Her revenge against Heracles. Selene "by the help of her magical charms filled a large chest full of

43

foam and froth, (known as *aphroselenos*, 'the foam of the Moon') out of which sprang an immense lion."

Certainly the use of foam in producing an offspring brings to mind the origins of Aphrodite who was also born of the foam of the ocean crashing against the shore (the masculine sea joining with the feminine Earth). And Selene, of course, did control the ocean tides.

It is also notable, as Moore puts forward, that here the Moon is producing a creature associated with the light of the Sun (which is the ruling Planet of Leo), that is, attempting to generating light Herself, rather than simply reflecting it. But the reality is that the Moon's light is surface only. And that attribute is reproduced in Her lion. He had the power of indestructibility, but only skin deep. When Heracles fought the lion in the first of his fabled Twelve Labours, he killed the lion by squeezing it to death and taking its indestructible hide for armour.

If the Moon, as the ruler of Cancer, represents all the inner self, your own true self that is normally hidden away, then White Moon Selena in Leo brings it out, bursting forth from behind the Cancerian shell. Like a mother giving birth, She produces the Lion out of all that She nurtured as strong and true within. Whether it was a 'natural' birth or a creation from Her foam, it scarcely matters. The Lion is the external representation of the true self within. And this external representation is indeed indestructible. White Moon Selena's Lion cannot be shaken out of its belief in its own self-image.

The White Shadow

As always, there's a shadow side. If one has a negative self-image, then that becomes externally expressed too. If you have inner issues of your own self-worth, then the Lion becomes the Mouse. Your insecurities are on display for all to see and they are just as unshakable as the Lion's strengths. Unlike with Cancer, a Leo can't hide behind a shell any more than a child can go back inside a mother's safe womb. This is the weakness of the Nemean Lion. If your inner self is vulnerable then Leo's White Moon Selena exposes your vulnerabilities to all the Heracles of the world.

A Hint of Shade

But if your inner self has been properly nurtured and you feel positive then this will shine for all to see. This is a profoundly magical ability. True belief in one's own self-image allows for tremendous powers of manifestation. It's power is to shine. Every day is one long affirmation. Thought becomes deed.

White Moon Selena in Virgo ♍

"With great power comes great responsibility"

— Stan Lee, *'Spider-Man' in Amazing Fantasy no.15, 1962*

The energy of Virgo leads us smoothly on from Leo's glitz and glamour and asks the question, "Now what?"

In Virgo, you take all of that shining power and look for a purpose. You feel a duty to be of some use; to be of service in this world. Whether it is to be an agent of change in society as a whole or being a carer to a loved one in need (or indeed *anyone* in need). A Virgo doesn't really distinguish whether what they do helps a thousand people all at once or individually, one at a time. The mere fact that they have a purpose and are serving is enough. The motive is pure.

And to successfully be of use they have to be good at what they do. The details need to be right. A doctor needs to go to medical school first, after all. Nobody is going to want your help if you are only guessing and will possibly just make things worse. The Virgo need for perfection in detail is always in service of making sure they can get it right when offering to help.

Purity, service and perfect attention to detail. The story of Selene and Endymion does resonate with these ideals. Selene, as the Moon, is a visible Goddess. She has Her job to do: to be seen in the sky, bringing illumination, controlling the tides, etc. So She is, by necessity, absent from most epic sagas of mythology. Or at least only takes a bit part. She's far too busy in service, up in the night sky. Her few nights off, She devotes to Her love life with Endymion.

Endymion himself can be seen as embodying the other qualities of Virgo. Pausanias wrote that Endymion "chose to sleep forever, remaining deathless and ageless", thus it can be said, remaining in an unchanging state of purity and perfection. In a rationalisation of the myths, a 3rd Century BCE contributor to the *Argonautica* of Apollonius of Rhodes wrote that Endymion was an astronomer who so devoted himself to the study of the heavens that he had to sleep by day. George Bean, in 1979, expanded on this with the suggestion that Endymion's studies were so detailed that he slept for thirty years.

Since the energy of Virgo, perfection and service, is so aligned with the concept of a 'highest aspiration' anyway, White Moon Selena has to take that Virgo energy even further. And the word that comes to mind is "superhero".

The drive for purity and perfection, which is par for the course for Virgo anyway, is supercharged by White Moon Selena to the point where you want to be the best there is in what you do. You don't do it for applause or for money, love or success. You do it because you have a purpose, indeed a responsibility to use your skills to be in service. Your work, in whatever form it takes, must be of use to society and the world as a whole. And your push to be the best, the most ideal representative of your chosen pursuit or profession, is in service to that most pure of ideals, a responsibility to be a positive force in this world.

It is not enough to be a doctor, you would aspire to be a consulting surgeon. It is not enough to be a judge, you would aim for the Supreme Court. If you are an entertainer, like an actor or singer, you would crave the biggest audience, not for the prestige or glamour, but purely for the honour of bringing pleasure and joy to the largest number of people.

The White Shadow

It would be easy to think that the shadow side to this is in asking, "But when do you find space to do something for yourself?". But that doesn't really apply to Virgo. Being of perfect service to others *is* doing something for yourself. That's how you feed your soul in Virgo.

No, the shadow is in the phrase 'not enough'. Throughout this book, the downside of White Moon Selena in any Sign is generally never quite being able to reach that highest aspiration. Generally you reach a point where you just have to settle and say, "That's as much as I can do" and you often reap a fair few rewards, one way or another, in getting as far as you did. But by its very nature, that's not really good enough for White Moon Selena in Virgo.

There is always further to go. No matter how high you climb, you may always have that nagging feeling that there is always going to be one more step you can take to be better in what you do, to be able to help more.

A Hint of Shade

To counter this drive to constantly do more, you need to turn your attention within and invoke the opposing Sign of Pisces. In the words of Lennon/McCartney, "Turn off your mind, relax and float downstream." Create a picture in your mind (or on paper if you are so inclined) of a world where nobody needs any more help from you. In your picture, you are the perfect expression of yourself and you have completed your soul's tasks. As you meditate, keep that feeling in your heart.

White Moon Selena in Libra

"I am Grey. I stand between the candle and the star. We are Grey. We stand between the darkness and the light."

— J. M. Straczynski, Babylon 5, 1994

Libra is the odd one out amongst the Air Signs. Both Aquarius and Gemini are both about chasing the new, whether it be in innovations or learning. Libra is about wanting to stand still.

Harmony, peace and balance are the keywords for Libra. Where there is strife, Libra wants to make peace. Where there is agitation, Libra wants to bring calm. It is the point of stillness between two extremes. Unsurprisingly, the Sun moves into Libra at an Equinox in mid-September. Irrespective of whether it is the Northern or Southern hemisphere, the hours of night and day are equal when Libra takes control of the sky.

However, it would be a mistake to think that Libra is all passivity. It can provoke quite intense action and force if necessary; but only to counter and cancel out an equal and opposite force coming in the other direction.

The highest aspiration of White Moon Selena in Libra is to create peace and harmony by whatever means possible; to seek the complete eradication of any conflict such that all is at rest.

Let us not forget that the Goddess Selene's perfect lover, Endymion was in a state of permanent sleep. The surviving fragments of the mythology do not reveal whether Selene loved

Endymion despite his slumber or *because* of it. All we know is that Endymion requested his state of endless sleep.

If this sounds a bit scary that's probably because it is. (It certainly scared me. The sinister implications only sunk in as I was in the middle of typing all this!). It is significant that the end of Libra's journey takes us to Scorpio, the Sign of the Underworld and death; the ultimate state of peace.

But if we set aside the end of the world or even sleeping forever as desirable aspirations(!) then we need to look for something a bit more personal. Not so much the creation of peace as the creation of balance and harmony.

More than just a straightforward work/life balance, the impact of White Moon Selena in Libra is to have *everything* in the mix; to assimilate every aspect and experience that life has to offer and blend them all into a melting pot. Unlike the shadow of White Moon Selena in Cancer where the need was to be all things to all people, in Libra you want to be all things to *yourself.* Love life, career, self-care regime, leisure, family, parenting; none of these things are to be compartmentalised to you. They all blend into one fulfilling, harmonious life.

The White Shadow

The main obstacle to creating perfect harmony is the constant annoyance of other people and their ideas and aims conflicting with yours. And unlike Selene, you do not have the luxury of only having to deal with people who are permanently asleep! This usually means you have to do a great deal of compromising in order to keep the peace. This may satisfy the Libra energies but will probably end up aggravating every other energy in you. How much are you supposed to compromise before you lose all sense of yourself?

A Hint of Shade

There comes a moment when guaranteeing 'peace in our time', as per Neville Chamberlain, stops working and you need to fight for peace. Invoke Aries energy to fight your corner and get the others in your life to make the compromises to fit in with *your* harmonies, rather than you fit in with theirs. Librans are capable of fighting very hard to create balance; but make the other side your target rather than yourself.

White Moon Selena in Scorpio   ♏

"This 'know yourself' is a saying not so big, but such a task Zeus alone of the gods understands"

— Ion of Chios (c480–421BC)

In late autumn, the illusion of holding on to perfect order falls away in the season of change. When Scorpio follows Libra, so comes the paradoxical realisation that the balance of order must itself be balanced by the swirl of chaos.

The mystical underworldly energies of Samhain and Hallowe'en wash over us under the gaze of Scorpio. The Scorpion's sting brings death to the Summer as we enter the months of darkness.

Libra strove to bring opposing sides together as equals and turning them into a harmonious whole. Scorpio revels in the opposition of dualities. Light and dark, order and chaos, death and rebirth. And Scorpio's energies lie, not in the balance, but in the transformation from one to the other.

A Scorpion digs beneath the surface and feeds off what lurks below. Scraping away the veneer of civilised society to reveal that which is considered taboo. Death, sex, the occult, dark magic: Scorpios will not blindly accept a taboo without taking the time to explore their own feelings about it.

A Scorpio understands death like no other Sign. After all, the Sign is in prominence during the season when nature dies away and goes into its Winter rest in the Northern Hemisphere. It understands that death is both inevitable and cyclical. In that endless cycle of death and rebirth, time becomes one great moment.

According to Apollonius' *Argonautica*, Endymion's eternal sleep and Selene's regular conjugal visits took place in a cave on Carian Mount Latmos. This is a liminal place; a place of transition between the light, being on a mountain, and the dark, being within the Earth. And there are no shortages of stories of sacred initiations taking place in caves within Greek mythology.

Scorpio lives in that initiatory moment of transition. It seeks that perfect understanding of all that has gone before and all that is to come and how all that combination of myriad potentials and experience boils down to one moment of existence: the here and now.

And in that precious moment, we shed all that no longer serves us. Whether that be old unfinished business that now seems unimportant, or future plans that feel like dead ends. Scorpio turns us inward to see what lies within. We connect with Selene's Underworld counterpart, Persephone, as we journey through our own personal Underworld. And in looking into the dark well of our souls we find White Moon Selena shining right back at us, leading us back out into Her Celestial Sphere, illuminating our Divine Selves.

With White Moon Selena in Scorpio, we are illuminated in our Underworld darkness within. We want no doubt inside us. We want to know ourselves with crystal clarity.

"Know Thyself" was inscribed on the Temple of Apollo in ancient Delphi, one of the most well-known of the Delphic maxims, the moral declarations prominently located in the temple. It has been examined and interpreted in many ways over the centuries, primarily by Plato who attributed it, in his *Socratic Dialogues*, to his mentor Socrates: "I investigate myself to know whether I am a monster more complicated and more furious than Typhon or a gentler and simpler creature, to whom a divine and quiet lot is given by nature."

With our natal White Moon Selena in Scorpio, we might end up spending hundreds of hours (and thousands of pounds) in therapy to find and understand our true core. We will uncover and reconcile every past trauma, major and minor, and examine every future goal to ascertain its worthiness. Only then can we truly feel able to enjoy the moment of now.

Because if we can understand all that lies within us, we can truly begin to understand what lies beneath the surface of the whole world that is around us. Look again at the above Plato quote. Is Socrates seeking to understand himself or humanity as a whole?

The White Shadow

Left unchecked, White Moon Selena in Scorpio looks under every rock to see what is crawling about under there. Nothing is what it appears to be. The surface of anything is a barrier to be breached. The darkness hides a secret truth and White Moon Selena will not tolerate darkness; it must be illuminated. Conspiracy theories may well be life's blood to White Moon Selena in Scorpio. No other Sign is so suited to vanishing down a rabbit hole to uncover sinister plots.

A Hint of Shade

Scorpios may have a fascination with bringing to the surface sexual taboos, but as Sigmund Freud never actually said, "sometimes a cigar is just a cigar".

To pull ourselves out of the deep well of obsession with uncovering that which hides in the dark, we need to invoke Taurus' ability to appreciate life and beauty for what it is. Watch the sunset from a comfortable chair and eat a well-prepared meal. Taureans appreciate 'the moment' just as much as Scorpios, but they know that something which is beautiful on the surface can still be enjoyed just for its beautiful surface. Do you really want to dig into the compost and fertiliser underneath, or do you just want to stop and smell the roses?

White Moon Selena in Sagittarius

"We choose to go to the Moon... We choose to go to the Moon in this decade and do the other things, not because they are easy, but because they are hard; because that goal will serve to organize and measure the best of our energies and skills"

— John Fitzgerald Kennedy, the Address at Rice University, September 12, 1962

Racing headlong towards the Solstice and the end of the calendar year, comes Sagittarius. The final Fire Sign in the Zodiac. Both Aries and Sagittarius are Signs of action and motion, but whereas Aries is about the destination, Sagittarius is about the journey.

New horizons are always in the sights of this most restless of Signs. Always looking for the greener grass on the other side of the hill. Or any colour grass, really... or any type of surface. All that matters is seeing and experiencing what's on the other side of the hill. And the next one. And the next one.

Sagittarius the Archer is the hunter that sets his sights on anything that is new or different and then devours it before moving on to the next target. Always collecting and assimilating new experiences in the interest of the Sagittarian's personal evolutionary journey.

The Goddess Selene had Her own evolutionary journey as time went on. Her story evolved until Her role as Moon Goddess was transformed into an aspect of Artemis, Goddess of the Hunt, with Her bow being symbolic of the Crescent Moon. Her time as Selene is not even the first stage of Her journey through mythology. There is evidence, found on a clay tablet excavated at Knossos in Crete, that She may previously have been known to the pre-Greece Cretans as the Goddess Mene.

It was around the 5th Century BCE that the god Apollo began to be identified with solar qualities and started assimilating the role of the visible Sun God Helios. As an inevitable consequence, Helios' sister Selene began to become more and more associated with Apollo's sister Artemis. And later still, the evolution continued into the Roman era as Artemis Herself became conflated with Diana.

Artemis the Huntress has no mythological tales related to the Moon, but Her virginity began to be reverse-engineered back into Selena's stories until Her relationship with Endymion became positively chaste.

The 4th Century CE Latin author Servius equates Diana with Hecate who had often been described as having three faces. He suggests a 'triple-faced Diana' with Luna in the celestial space, Artemis on the Earth and Hecate in the underworld. He also suggested that Goddess of childbirth Lucina represented the waxing moon; Diana, the full moon; and Hecate, the waning phase. It is this depiction of the three Goddess phases that led to Robert Graves' 20th Century depiction of the 'Triple Goddess', represented by the Triple Moon.

Steve Moore is dismissive of attempts to "back project" modern neo-pagan beliefs backwards, claiming, "We live in a world that would rather have neat-and-tidy versions of ancient myths than the 'difficult' complexity of having to deal with the ancient sources." However Moore does concede that the Triple Moon Goddess has Her place as a valid symbolism for contemporary beliefs.

The evolution of Mene into Selene, into Artemis and Diana, into the Triple Moon Goddess is the energy of Sagittarius in action. The Moon Goddess does not stay static. Her story plays out according to the archetypal needs of Her followers and worshippers and as those needs change, so does She.

White Moon Selena in Sagittarius brings a need for evolution. The highest aspiration in this Sign in is to transform yourself; to always believe you can do better and be better. An ongoing desire to reinvent yourself and effectively become a new person. Like suddenly feeling a need to quit your job, leave your spouse and go live in an Ashram. Until, before long, you move on to a new country and go to university. And then marry someone else. Life becomes a pilgrimage to your own personal equivalent of Nirvana, when there will be no more desire because you will ultimately have experienced and understood everything. And you believe that every step on this journey will change you.

Until finally you reach the point, seven years (there's that number again) after Kennedy's speech when Neil Armstrong makes "a giant leap for mankind."

The White Shadow

The problem with continually moving on is that you always leave footprints. The partner you leave behind; the unfinished work; the children that still need their parent. You can't always drop everything and move on. Not without sometimes leaving chaos in your wake. There is seldom such a thing as a clean break. And the grass may be different on the other side, but not always greener. New experiences can bring suffering as well as enlightenment. The challenge to those with White Moon Selena in Sagittarius is to look before you leap and how to leap without leaving devastation in your wake.

A Hint of Shade

In the 21st century, the new age of Aquarius, the restless Sagittarian can employ all of Gemini's tools to explore the world and beyond without leaving your sofa. Watch, listen, read and learn about new worlds and civilisations through films, books and the internet. But even if you do answer that call for literally moving, travelling and evolving, taking the time for communication will help soften the impacts; both for yourself in learning about the new worlds you are going to (geographically and/or metaphorically) and for others in your old world that you may be wanting to leave behind.

White Moon Selena in Capricorn ♑

"I'd spent nearly sixty years trying to hide how competitive I was, and it didn't work anyway, so why didn't I just own it? I am competitive. I want to be the best. I want to pursue excellence every day of my life.",

— Erwin Raphael McManus, *The Way of the Warrior*, 2019

The final Earth Sign of the Zodiac year is the Sign that welcomes in the new calendar year. The Sagittarian journey is over and it is time to take root. It is a Sign that strips away all accumulated baggage of sentimentality, abstractions and ego and leaves you with the bare essential necessities to work without distraction.

The Capricorn, seen from the perspective of the Northern hemisphere, takes the bare seed, buried under the frozen earth and makes it sprout. During the Capricorn month it stays hidden away and is doing all its work underground in the dark, unseen and unheralded.

Capricorn is certainly a Sign of ambition and dedication, but there's a purity to it too. Capricorns tend not to have ulterior motives for their actions, they pursue their ambitions with efficiency because they believe that what they are doing is right. If they are ruthless in seeking promotion at work it is because they want the opportunity to achieve more and do it better. Money and power is a consequence of their ambition, not the reason for it.

As discussed in the Virgo chapter, Selene is a visible goddess. She is not hidden away behind stories and legends and archetypes.

She is *there*. She is hanging in the sky every night as a tangible physical presence. Like Her brother, Helios the Sun and Her sister, Eos the Dawn, Selene *is* fully what She represents. These three siblings have the Capricorn value of integrity. They are the epitome of 'what you see is what you get'.

Furthermore, Moore points out that Selene had no particular cult following. As Moon Goddess She had no temples or particular places of worship. There were no 'Festivals of Selene'. She had no need of any of that. If anyone did 'worship' Her, as I am sure many did, they came to Her on *Her* terms; under Her moonlight whenever She happened to be up there, getting on with Her job.

This purity of purpose and integrity is inherent in the qualities of White Moon Selena in Capricorn shows you *your* purity and integrity. We do not simply consider the world of work here, it is whatever your calling is. It could be in service, in learning, as a homemaker or as a rebel with a cause. With White Moon Selena in Capricorn you will strive to succeed and be the best in what you seek to do. Not for the rewards it gives but because you truly believe to your core, within the very roots of your soul that it is the right thing for you to do.

The White Shadow

"No one is more dangerous than he who imagines himself pure in heart: for his purity, by definition, is unassailable," wrote James Baldwin, in an essay in *Esquire* in 1961. Left unchecked, the Capricorn-White Moon Selena can become isolated in self-righteousness. Ruthlessness can be self-justified by a belief that is for the 'greater good'. The most monstrous dictators and villains are all 'heroes' of their own stories.

A Hint of Shade

It is not enough to 'know' you are right and pure. You have to feel it too. A healthy emotional life away from your core activity provides a healthy work-life balance. Even the visibly dedicated Goddess Selene took a couple of days off every month to 'go dark' and pursue Her love life with Endymion. Indulge in the joys of Cancer by taking time out to do something fun that just makes you happy.

ᴄWhite ᴏ℧oon Ꮪelena in ᴀquarius   ꙮꙮ

"I don't want to belong to any club that would have me as a member."

— Groucho Marx, Groucho and Me, 1959

The final Air Sign in the Zodiac Cycle is the Water Carrier. This so often confuses people into thinking Aquarius is a Water Sign. And that suits Aquarius just fine. Aquarians hate to be tied down and defined. They are above such labels. Above everything in fact.

They are renowned as the rebellious free thinkers of all the Signs. That is not to say they are out to lead a revolution, smash the system and change the world. Changing others is just as much anathema to Aquarians as being forced to change themselves.

All Aquarians want is to be free to do their own thing in their own way, thinking their own thoughts and feeling their own truths. They will challenge longstanding assumptions, break rules that do not fit their own individual worldview and thoroughly celebrate being different.

It is often said that Aquarians have that touch of genius. It doesn't mean they are any more intelligent than anyone else, just that they are apt to see connections and have ideas that simply would never occur to anyone else. These ideas can just as easily be wrong as right but either way they are likely ideas that have never been thought of before. Their ideas may well inspire change in those around them, even if they have no desire to lead them.

It can certainly be said that the Goddess Selene went Her own way. Despite the fact that the myths of many goddesses of the period, including other Moon Goddesses such as Artemis, have had associations with traditional archetypes of womanhood, notably the maiden-mother-crone archetypes, Selene has tended to avoid such associations. Nor has Selene been counted amongst any goddesses celebrated during the religious festivals celebrated by women of the time, or any religious or cult practice at all, that we know of.

It seems the defining attribute of Selene is a complete inability to be defined. The ancient writers and historians of the Classical Era, Hesiod, Hyginus, Homer, Euripides and Diodorus Siculus all cite completely different accounts of Selene's origins. And in that Eleventh House attribute of seeking out people of a similar type, Selene's lover Endymion also refuses to be defined; is he astronomer, shepherd or prince?

White Moon Selena in Aquarius brings highest aspirations that are unique and defy categorisation. You will have no ambitions to climb the career ladder, be the highest rank or the best whatever. You will want to do or be something that nobody has ever done before or would never even think of doing. This makes it difficult for me to give examples, because my White Moon Selena *isn't* in Aquarius! It might involve inventing a whole new medium of art in the Fifth House; finding a hitherto undiscovered niche of self-employed career in the Tenth House; and I would not want to speculate on the type of relationships you would aspire to in the Seventh House!

The White Shadow

The challenge for White Moon Selena in Aquarius is probably contrariness and an inability to compromise. You could find yourself struggling to move forward in your journey and someone comes along and makes a suggestion as to how to proceed. It could be a very good idea that has every chance of working well. But it wasn't *your* idea. You wanted to do it your way, overcoming the challenges in your own unique and innovative way. It spoils it if you've needed someone else's answer. The Aquarian energy can be too stubborn for its own good.

A Hint of Shade

To counteract the stubborn Aquarian energy, you need to invoke some Leo and play to the crowd. The Leo love of self-expression harmonises with Aquarius very well. Showing off your individuality doesn't compromise it. But it will invite a little adulation (possibly a little ridicule too, but most Aquarians are used to that and hardly care). Adulation and positive reinforcement might irritate the stubborn Aquarian's need to be different, and certainly an Aquarian doesn't want or need followers, but all that positive energy, reinforcing your belief in yourself, can kickstart the genius juices.

White Moon Selena in Pisces ♓

"One realized all sorts of things. The value of an illusion, for instance, and that the shadow can be more important than the substance"

— Jean Rhys CBE, Quartet, 1928

And now we come to the final Sign in the Great Star Wheel: Pisces. I'd really like to say we are finishing on a high, but that doesn't apply here as Pisces is deep... really deep! Even so, beyond all other Signs, this is the one where the 'imaginary' Moon of the Spiritual realms thrives best.

Pisces thrives in the worlds of the divine. During this month, when Winter is ending but not-ended and Spring is starting but not-started, the dividing line between fantasy and reality is at its blurriest. In this liminal state, neither one nor the other, the Piscean moves through the world through the filter of dreams.

Pisces is, of course, a Water Sign. How could it be anything else, being the Fish? In this Sign you go swimming through the depths of your subconscious and imagination.

The Latin poet Claudian wrote in around the late 4th century, quoted in *De Raptu Proserpinae*, that Selene (as Luna) was fostered by the sea Goddess Tethys, the wife of Ocean. It suggests how White Moon Selena's influence was nurtured by the influence of waters, expressed in the astrological context by Pisces and Neptune. (And we know, of course, that the Moon returns this nurturing love through her tending to the tides).

So Pisces energy is therefore highly nurturing of White Moon Selena. The ability to believe and have faith in something ostensibly illusory and spiritual lives and thrives in the watery depths of the Sign of the fishes.

The *Homeric Hymn XXII – To Selene* refers to Her rising "having bathed her lovely body in the waters of Ocean" which in those days was envisioned as a great stream circling the edges of the flat Earth. And in *The Odyssey*, Homer tells us that beyond the Ocean Stream is where dreams live. Moore reasons that it is quite appropriate for Selene to commence her nocturnal journey from the place of dreams having bathed in the energies of dreaming.

As discussed in the Gemini chapter, Selene had a role in antiquity as a dream oracle. The shrine to Pasiphae, a title attributed by Pausanias to Selene, near Thalamae being the most notable example. Visitors would sleep in one of her shrines, or similar temples dedicated to other oracles, to receive Her divine messages in their dreams.

To have White Moon Selena in Pisces is to be 'living the dream'. You thoroughly embrace the fantasies of your dream life. The illusion of living your highest aspiration is alluring. Fantasising about it can be so satisfying that it almost doesn't matter that it might not be real. The Pisceans don't need to live in the mundane real world, the Pisceans live in the world that they *perceive* it to be.

On one level, of course, we all relate to the world though our perceptions. We see what our eyes 'tell' us we see and our brain interprets that data accordingly. But how is our brain doing the interpreting? A Taurean will take the data literally; in a 'that's what I see so that's how it is' view on the world. A Piscean brain works with quite a different approach. They will take the data from the senses and construct elaborate structures in the deep ocean of their souls of what they *believe* the world is, or *should* be. And then they relate to that subjective image instead. They don't believe what they see, they see what they believe.

A person with White Moon Selena in Pisces will see their highest aspiration, their divine self, and quite naturally have the ability to see themselves in that divine form, or at least believe that it is a highly attainable goal. Their inner self-image is thoroughly overlaid with the fantasy and a faith that this inner self can naturally exist in the outer world too. After all, in the world according to Pisces, there is no real distinction between the inner subjective construct of the world and the outer objective one.

On the plus side, embracing the self-illusion can work quite an effective glamour. Believing that the world sees you in the same idealised way you see yourself inevitably gives you the aura of confidence and success. And any assertiveness trainer will tell you that if you have that aura of confidence, the world around you really does see it and buy into it. Belief plus intention is the source of magical power and manifestation, after all. Or, to put it another way, 'Fake it til you Make it!'

Ultimately, if you believe wholeheartedly in your highest divine dream self then the world around you will perceive it and believe it too. And that power of shared belief may well attract the manifestation of your White Moon Selena highest aspiration without you even trying that hard. The energy of Pisces is the power that brings Tinkerbell back to life when Peter asks the audience to wish really, really hard!

But, of course it isn't that easy. It will likely rely on other Signs and Planets being in the right pattern. To believe in the fantasy is all Pisces, but you'd probably need the right placements in Leo to be able to project the belief outwards.

If you aren't able to effectively project your divine fantasy self-image outwards (perhaps you retreat behind a shell of Cancer) then you may well find yourself falling under the shadow side of Pisces.

The White Shadow

Living in a self-indulgent fantasy life can be very addictive if you are not able to externalise and use your imagination positively. This may lead you to neglect the realities of life, indulging in the false luxury of escapism. This illusory life can seldom last long when your dreams are confronted by harsh reality, especially if there are Earth Signs in your chart that are pulling at you. Unfulfilled dreams and unexpressed fantasy often results in despondency, despair and perhaps depression. And Pisces can provide a very deep dark well for depressions to fall into.

A Hint of Shade

As said above, the realities signified by Earth Signs does not sit well with Piscean fantasy, but invoking Virgo in particular can soften the hard falls back to reality. The Virgo attention to detail suggests taking baby steps towards Earth. Make a short 'to-do' list every day with a few practical tasks that need to be done in between the daydreaming.

7. The Pull of the Planets

The one thing that all physical planetary bodies have in common is gravity. They all exert a pull on each other to one extent or another. It is how they maintain their orbital patterns.

They exert a pull on each other in astrology too, as they 'orbit' your astrological charts. This 'pull' is referred to as an 'aspect' and relate to the angles of their respective positions.

Sometimes they overlap and appear in the same place in the sky, called a conjunction; combining their power. Then they can be in opposite ends of the sky with their energies pulling away from each other.

The elemental forces of the Signs also come into play:

- If two Planets are in two Signs of the same element, for example, Water Signs Pisces and Cancer, 120 degrees apart, they are in a 'Trine' and their energies peacefully harmonise.
- If they are in supporting elements like an Air Sign and a Fire Sign, such as Aquarius and Aries, they are in 'Sextile', 60 degrees apart, and excite and stimulate each other.
- But if they are in disharmonious elemental Signs at 90 degrees to each other, like watery Pisces and airy Gemini or fiery Sagittarius, then they are 'Squared' and the energies will refuse to play together.

(There are other types of aspect, but they exert a lesser 'pull' and their effect on White Moon Selena is fairly negligible, for all intents and purposes.)

If two or more Planets are in an aspect to your White Moon Selena at the time of your birth, i.e. in your natal chart, then the effect is ongoing throughout your life, whether that will be a soft supporting effect, a stimulating exciting effect or one that might pose some challenges. ('A sweet or spicy seasoning added to your birth chart meal' as I described it in Chapter 4.)

If a Planet's current position moves into an aspect with where your White Moon Selena was at your birth, then this is a transiting aspect and its effect lasts for the length of time it takes for the current Planet to move out of range.

When the current position of White Moon Selena moves into a transiting aspect with one of your natal planetary positions then the effect on your divine self and highest aspirations is similar.

Calculating when these transits occur and their effect is the basis for horoscope predictions.

There are many more 'Planets' in our Solar System than I have included in this book, including minor and dwarf planets in the outer reaches like Chiron, Eris and Sedna. But I have concentrated on the major, most established Planets to prevent the book from becoming too unwieldy. And the astrological effect on White Moon Selena of the most remote ones can be considered relatively minor.

Similarly, I have not included an examination of the other 'Moon Ghosts' like Black Moon Lilith, the North/South Nodes, Light Moon Arta and Priapus as they could probably take up a whole book in themselves.

The Sun

There's a good reason why, when we are asked what 'our Sign' is, we always fall back on what Sign the Sun was in on our birth chart. The Sun is the source of pretty much all light and power in our Solar System (hence the name: 'system of the Sun'). And as an astrological 'Planet' it shows us the source of our own power within; the traits that define our true selves.

This makes for an extremely illuminating clash when our true selves, our ego, as defined by the Sun, come into aspect with our highest divine selves, as defined by White Moon Selena. When the sunlight shines over our White Moon Selena power, our relationship with our divine selves and highest aspirations become highlighted.

This poses questions, about whether we are aligned with our highest selves? Or are our highest aspirations to pull away from our true selves?

A very down to Earth Sun-Taurean may feel never quite settled due to a White Moon Selena-Sagittarius need to evolve or grow. A Sun-Aquarian rebel without a cause may feel a 10th House White Moon Selena aspiration for high status and recognition in their field (their own unique field, of course!)

It can, of course, be seen as a sibling rivalry in our charts. Helios, the Sun is Selene's brother, after all. Brothers and Sisters clash all the time, with each one wanting to outshine the other. But ultimately their respective influences fall into alignment and they pull together as a family; your true self and ego finds a path that leads you towards your divine self.

The Sun in Conjunction with White Moon Selena

When these two powers work together, you know you are on the right path. In many ways you feel you are already there, for all intents and purposes. Even if your life is not precisely where your highest aspirations want you to be, you can envision yourself there and you can feel your divine self right there inside you.

If this conjunction is in your natal chart then you will tend to identify with and embody your divine self. You live as though you have already achieved your goals and it is only a matter of time before the rest of the world catches up with any remaining pesky details.

The Sun in Opposition to White Moon Selena

With these powers in opposition, the Earth standing between the two puts one in the shadow. You can follow the dictates of your ego or you can strive towards your divine self. But while this Opposition is in force, you will likely find that circumstances will prevent you from being able to do both. Whichever path you choose right now will not feel wholly fulfilling but will still be right for you in its own way.

If this opposition is in your natal chart then you are going to often feel that you are pulled in a direction contrary to your nature. Striving for your highest aspirations and just being yourself may well be something you are going to have to take turns in doing. Follow your ego during a Solar Return and your divine calling during a Solar Opposition and things will work out.

The Sun Squared with White Moon Selena

With this aspect in play, there is such a friction between the Sun and White Moon Selena that your need to follow your aspirations may be preventing you from acting in accordance with your true nature and, in turn, the suppression of your ego hinders your ability to strive towards your divine self. You are stuck in a Catch-22 during this period. You may be able to break the impasse by invoking Aquarius (or see where your Uranus is right now) and deliberately do something completely out of character.

If this Square is in your natal chart, there is likely to be a complete incompatibility between who you are and what you aspire to be. For example, the jazz pianist who longs to play classical (and vice versa). The skills and mindset that make you good at one can often actively prohibit you from doing the other. The two selves cannot be resolved, you can only be true to your Sun-self. Being your absolute best Sun-self cannot help but being divine in its own way. And when your current Sun moves into Conjunction with White Moon Selena, it may shine a light on a more compatible way to strive towards your divine self.

The Sun in Trine with White Moon Selena

This harmonious aspect can be very confusing to your self-image. You may not be entirely certain which is your true self and which is your divine self. The result is usually that you think you are striving towards becoming your divine self but actually you are just doing what comes naturally for your ego. It might ultimately be the same thing, more or less, but it could just leave you with a slightly inflated ego while this aspect is in effect.

If this aspect is in your natal chart then you may well have a natural tendency to have an over-inflated ego. You may even feel that your highest aspirations lie, more or less, where you happen to be. When the current Sun moves into conjunction with your natal White Moon Selena, you will feel the wake up call and give yourself a kick back in the right direction.

The Sun in Sextile with White Moon Selena

This stimulating aspect may bring inspiration in how to develop your true self and ego expression in a manner that will bring you closer to your aspirations. You begin to see connections and pathways that may not have existed before or been hidden. While the Sextile is in effect, the Sun acts like a huge flashing light bulb over your head giving you fresh ideas and intuitive leaps.

If this aspect is in your natal chart then it may reveal a talent for self-development and continuous growth. A clear insight into your divine potential provides stimulation for your ego, which in turn pushes you ever closer to your aspirations.

ᘔhe ᙢoon

The physical form of Selene Herself, the Moon is held to be second only to the Sun in astrological power. And there is no small amount of people who might place Her in primary position.

She is the planetary ruler of Cancer which is wholly appropriate, given the Moon's control over the world's tides. The Moon is the domain of our emotional responses, our feelings. Where She fits in our natal chart shows us where we are most emotionally sensitive in our lives. Where do we feel the most joy? Where are we most vulnerable to sorrow? Where do we get downright touchy and irritable?

In Aries your greatest source of joy and grief may be dependent on whether you win or lose in competition. An 11th House placement indicates your happiness may be related to being around friends and likeminded people.

I have referred to it before, but here it is necessary to stress that Selene is not only the Goddess of the Moon, She was believed to be the Moon itself. In the same way that Her brother Helios is the Sun, Her father Hyperion is the Sky and, most famously, Her grandmother Gaia is the Earth. They are all called 'visible gods' who existed as physical presence in our reality and not in some spiritual home like Olympus.

As a side note, it throws new light on the ritual of 'Drawing Down the Moon' in practicing magic. To do so is to 'draw down' Selene Herself; something not to be taken lightly. Apollonius of Rhodes wrote of the sorceress Medea whose powers involved Drawing Down the Moon. Selene was apparently a little irritated at being drawn away from Her duties and, more importantly,

Her conjugal time with Endymion in order to empower Medea. She said, "Oft times with thoughts of love I have been driven away by thy crafty spells in order that in the darkest of night thou might work thy sorcery at ease."

So if you do practice this ritual in your own magical work, be mindful of what you might be interrupting in Selene's routine!

Selene's astrological influence as the Moon itself is, as I said, considerable enough as the mistress of our feelings, but Her influence extends beyond Her physical domain. She also has Her spiritual, shadow and echo selves that make themselves known in our charts; all the 'virtual moons' and points defined by Her orbital path such as the Nodes, Black Moon Lilith, Priapus, Light Moon Arta and or course White Moon Selena, Selene's echo incarnation through a Gate of Eternity into the spiritual realms.

There is not enough space in this volume to consider all the relationships between White Moon Selena and all of the Moon's other echo points and selves. But White Moon Selena connection with Her physical incarnation brings significant differences, compared to other Planets, in considering the effect of aspects.

White Moon Selena in Conjunction with the Moon – The Eclipse

The Moon rotates around the Earth every 28–29 days moving from New phase to Full to Dark. At some point within this month, it moves in front of, that is, in *conjunction* to White Moon Selena. Not being physically in our reality, Selena doesn't have phases, as such. Not as we know them. But Selena is being shadowed by the Moon at that moment, thus disrupting our reception of White Moon Selena's energies.

So we are going to feel *something* going on in our connection to our divine aspirations. Certainly, the Sign that White Moon Selena and the Moon are moving through at the time of the conjunction will be one component of this phenomenon, but also the phase of the Moon on that day will also be significant.

Obviously the effect will be emotional. That's the level the Moon works on. And the very nature of an eclipse, shadowing and blocking light and energy, I feel, is going to provoke a sense of loss. So a White Moon Selena/Moon Conjunction is going to result in a sense of loss and being directionless. We will, for those few hours, lose touch with our goals and, on some level, question their importance.

And the phase The Moon is showing is going to shape those feelings of loss.

Here's how those conjunctions might show up and distract us from our highest aspirations for a while:

When the conjunction is in your natal chart, the effect is likely to numb your emotional connection to your highest aspirations. This is not to say you won't feel the pull of your divine self, it is just that your emotional responses and joy will be in dealing with other aspects of your journey rather than in the striving for fulfilment. And, again, the phase of the moon at the time of your birth will be a factor in where your emotional responses will be redirected.

New Moon

That beautiful new crescent appearing in the sky is the ultimate expression of "oh look, it's a shiny thing!" It's the energy of distraction. At this time our aspirations are diverted towards new and different pursuits: the good; the bad; and the harmless. It doesn't really matter which of the three it is, the important thing is that it will take your eye off the ball. Long term high aspirations are obscured by the seductive lure of new, exciting and relatively petty distractions. Still, they'll be fun. And we all need a break from long term striving.

A New Moon-White Moon Selena eclipse in your natal chart you are likely to get more satisfaction from a number of short-term aspirations rather than one long term one.

Full Moon

The Full Moon is the Mother ready to give birth. It is the time to manifest our projects. Our highest aspirations are subsumed by the here and now. White Moon Selena's energies no longer drive us forward to our future and our attentions become focused totally on the present. It is a highly productive and energetic few days as you tick things off your to-do list, but you may feel you are just doing 'busy-work' and that nothing is going to be particularly consequential. But no completed project is ever meaningless. Completing the final level on that computer game may not be your highest aspiration but if it makes you feel good to accomplish it, then it is still a plus for you.

A Full Moon-White Moon Selena eclipse in your natal chart may well bring a strong gift for mindfulness work. You will enjoy living for the day and getting the most satisfaction and fulfilment when you, as Kipling put it, "fill the unforgiving minute with sixty seconds worth of distance run".

Crescent Moon

The waning crescent is the moment for letting go of the old. This is normally a good thing. Every so often, we all have to do some 'house clearing' in our lives to make space for the new. The waning crescent provides good energetic help in doing that. But when the

Moon is eclipsing White Moon Selena during this phase, you have to be careful you are not throwing out the proverbial baby with the bathwater. It is a time when you come to doubt what your highest aspirations really are and may be tempted to turn away from them. Questioning your goals and destiny are good things and can help make them stronger but unless you've got a Selena Return birthday going on, wait a few days until the phase changes and the eclipse passes before making any hasty decisions.

A Crescent Moon-White Moon Selena eclipse in your natal chart gives you a strong taste for the minimalist life. Your satisfaction comes less from striving for your highest aspirations, but more from decluttering your life of everything else.

Dark Moon

In many witchcraft circles, the dark night between the vanishing waning crescent and the emergent new moon is a night off from spiritual work. The magical Moon energy is switched off because the Goddess Selene is off for an assignation with Endymion. When this dark phase conjuncts White Moon Selena, you might even forget what your highest aspirations are. It is literally a 'Dark Night of the Soul' when you have not the slightest inkling of what you are here for and what you are supposed to do with your life. Take heart that this phase generally only lasts one or two nights and think of it more as a spiritual holiday. Our highest aspirations can cope with a night off.

A Dark Moon-White Moon Selena eclipse in your natal chart brings with it a sense of indifference to your highest aspirations. You are still likely to feel a pull towards it but may not feel much emotional resonance in whether you are achieving it or not. This is not necessarily a bad thing as a big part of our relationship with White Moon Selena is how we cope with *not* reaching our highest aspirations. And being fairly nonchalant with where we end up on our journey is not a bad state to be in.

Other Aspects

The other aspects between the Moon and White Moon Selena are more straightforward than a present conjunction as there is no eclipse effect to account for. But it is still worth considering any possible distinctions in effect, depending on whether the current Moon phase is New, Full or Dark. It is also worth noting that there is a considerable difference in whether the current, slow moving White Moon Selena is transiting your natal Moon or if the current fast-moving Moon is transiting your natal White Moon Selena. In the former the effect lasts about seven weeks whereas with the latter effect will come and go in about 12 hours.

White Moon Selena in Conjunction to the natal Moon, or the Moon in Conjunction to the natal White Moon Selena

With this alignment in effect, your happiness is your compass to illumination. Your emotional wellbeing is interwoven with your journey towards your highest self. Working towards your highest aspirations brings you happiness and, conversely, anything you do that makes you happy is, in some way, bringing you closer to your divine state.

White Moon Selena in Opposition to the Moon

This polarising aspect can lead to questioning whether striving for your highest aspirations is actually fulfilling. Simply put, are you enjoying it or is the lack of fulfilment getting you down?

If this opposition is in your natal chart you may well be a bit of a 'glass half empty' type of personality. Your emotional responses with regard to your highest aspirations are more focused on sadness over what you have not achieved rather than joy at your successes. But overcoming frustration can be as strong a motivator as attaining happiness and you can still find pleasure in the House where your Moon actually *is*.

White Moon Selena Squared with the Moon

This conflicted aspect suggests that you might make better progress towards your aspirations if you take emotion out of the equation. Right now your emotional responses to situations, whether positive or negative, are counterproductive and distracting. When you need to focus on your highest aspirations, you may be better off moving with your head rather than your heart.

If this aspect is in your natal chart you are likely more of a planner and thinker when it comes to your aspirations. Emotions are all well and good, and they certainly have their place in other sides of your life, but it is a clear head that brings progress in your divine path.

White Moon Selena in Trine with the Moon

With this harmonising aspect in effect, you are apt to follow your Moon's placement for positive emotional responses with an expectation that your aspirations will take care of themselves. But this is not like a conjunction; it is not going to work automatically. However, if you actively channel your good vibrations right now in the direction of your divine self, you will likely get a boost in your progress.

If this aspect is in your natal chart then you will likely have more of an optimistic 'glass half full' approach to your aspirations. And any progress you make towards your highest aspirations will tend to feedback into a positive approach to other areas of your life too.

White Moon Selena in Sextile with the Moon

With this stimulating aspect working for you, you tend to be able to make better progress towards your divine self whenever you feel a dynamic emotional response in other areas of your life. It will matter little whether the response is positive or negative, as long as it is forceful; anger will generate just as much motivation as joy for the Sextile to activate for you.

If this aspect is in your natal chart then emotional stimulation in your life is likely to be a strong motivating factor in your making progress towards your highest aspirations. Passionate love, joy and anger will propel you towards your divine self; sorrow, bliss and peaceful comfort will likely cause stagnation.

Mercury

Mercury is the fleet footed messenger of the gods. In our sky He races a dross the Zodiac faster than anything (apart from the Moon) and will meet up, in one aspect or another, with another Planet every few days. You would think that makes Him the ultimate gossip but that would only be while He's racing through Gemini. As the God of Thieves He can be quite discreet with ferreting out secrets too.

Mercury is the ruling Planet of both Gemini and Virgo so if anything can characterise Mercury it is accuracy of information. He sees on every level. Powering Gemini, His eyes are wide angled, capturing as much information as possible across wide vistas. Powering Virgo, He is a zoom lens, capturing that data in the minutest detail. Never being too far away from the Sun, everything is exposed to the light of day.

Being in rapid, almost constant communication with all the other Planets, Mercury could be the energy that makes astrological aspects and transits work. Without social butterfly Mercury, the Planets would keep themselves to themselves and might never talk to their neighbours.

Mercury is also known as one of the trickster gods and this is never more apparent than when Mercury goes retrograde. Whether gossipy or discreet, Mercury is always truthful. Well the message may not always be the truth but the messenger will transmit it truthfully. However when He is retrograde, the Trickster side to Him comes to the fore.

Retrograde is when the Planet appears to change direction in the sky and moves backwards through the Signs. It is an illusion, of course, created by the Planets moving at different speeds. It is like when you overtake another car on the motorway and it appears to be going backwards relative to your own speed. But illusion is the stock in trade of the Trickster God.

The message stays the same but the transmission becomes garbled. It becomes a riddle to solve, a code to break before the message is revealed.

The first evidence of the effects of Mercury retrograde date back in oral tradition to the 1960s, according to Susanna Crockford's 2018 academic paper on the subject, but it started to became widely acknowledged in the astrological world in the 1980s when computers in data processing became widespread. And it became noticeable that errors and system crashes were more common during the weeks of Mercury retrograde. An American newsletter called *Mercury Hour*, founded in 1974, canvassed readers to write in with their problems and respondents would often cite Mercury retrograde as a cause.

In our heads, Mercury is data retrieval. It is the ability to the ability to summon up facts from the deep recesses of our memories when we are asked a question. It strives for impartial accuracy but it is the effect of other Planets aspecting Mercury that provide filters, for good or ill.

The Sun's effect on Mercury will interpret facts through our ingrained prejudices. Venus will cause our memories to be seen through the proverbial rose-tinted glasses. Jupiter reinterprets and reframes our memories of events to make us look or feel better.

White Moon Selena illuminates and brings crystal clear total and dispassionate recall and perfect powers of observation.

Mercury in Conjunction with White Moon Selena

Never play Trivial Pursuit with someone when Mercury is in conjunction with White Moon Selena. The mind is clear of fog and the synapses between memory and consciousness become the proverbial information super-highway. The result is that you could be a sparkling after-dinner speaker with anecdotes on your lips for every topic. But you could also be the crashing bore of any social gathering. Does anyone really need to hear all the history of agriculture in Columbia when the question was simply "How do you like your coffee?"

If you have this aspect in your birth chart then you may be well suited to the acting profession as memorising a script is likely to come naturally to you.

Mercury in Opposition to White Moon Selena

When Mercury is in opposition to White Moon Selena, you may feel a contrary need to debate. All ideas are susceptible to a different point of view and you can not only see it, but may feel a constant pull to express it. Your mantra becomes "But on the other hand..." It is not that you are necessarily disagreeing with everyone, it is just working to the theory that debating alternate takes on an idea can help bring clarity and understanding to the topic being discussed.

If you have this aspect in your birth chart then you may have a tendency to be indecisive in your opinions and possibly be considered a bit 'wishy washy'. Even if you can see both sides, sometimes you have to stop sitting on the fence and take a stand on one side or the other.

Mercury Squared with White Moon Selena

With Mercury in this aspect to White Moon Selena it is a bit like wearing blinkers. You believe you know all you need to know.

You come to feel you have a firm grip on your world viewpoints at this time. Your ideas and opinions are fairly fixed and you are entirely comfortable with them. You are certain you are right. So if Mercury knocks at your door, delivering a message that does not fit your world view, you are not likely to take it well. An Ariean will argue. A Taurean will put fingers in their ears, singing "La, La, La". An Aquarian will probably stick to their point even if they know they are wrong, just to be bloody-minded. But no-one with this aspect is going to just accept it.

If this aspect is in your natal chart then you are likely to be quite stubborn in your opinions. New facts need to received and interpreted to conform to your established opinions.

Mercury in Trine with White Moon Selena

When Mercury is in this harmonious trine with White Moon Selena, it is time when you are likely to be extremely receptive to ideas and information put to you. Not to put too fine a point to it, the word that comes to mind is 'gullible'! Your filters are switched off and your eagerness to learn and take in everything around you means you are open to lies and falsehoods as much as you are to truth.

If this aspect is in your natal chart then you learn and assimilate facts and knowledge very easily. But you may have a tendency to be a bit too trusting and will believe everything you hear.

Mercury in Sextile with White Moon Selena

With Mercury excited by White Moon Selena, it stimulates your natural curiosity to the utmost. Every fact you take in just leaves you wanting to learn more, drilling down to the tiniest detail. This is an example of the 'zoom lens' side of Mercury. If something grabs your interest, you will meet it eagerly and want to stick with it until you've exhausted every facet of the topic.

If this aspect is in your natal chart then you are apt to be an excellent student in subjects that interest you. You may not get very many GCSEs at school, but you may well pursue at least one of them to PhD level.

Venus

♀

Call Her Aphrodite; call Her Ishtar; call Her Innana. By any other name, Venus is the Goddess of Love. And in our sky She dances around the Sun, like She's drawing the petals of a Rose.

Her Planet, as the ruler of both Taurus and Libra, evokes the desire for both beauty and harmony in your chart. And both of these, when combined, are essential components of our love lives. We seek the harmony of togetherness and completion in love. And that which we love is generally beautiful to our own eyes.

Both Selene and Endymion were both considered extremely beautiful in mythology. And having one partner being permanently asleep certainly makes the relationship harmonious if nothing else (especially since it didn't seem to affect his potency, and there's no record of Selene having any complaint!)

Where Venus appears around your chart tends to indicate how you live your love life. Do you crave passion (Aries) or intellectual stimulation (Gemini)? Are you faithful and dependable (Taurus) or do you keep an eye open for better prospects (Sagittarius)?

Whichever Sign and House Venus lives in, the power of White Moon Selena when She appears in your transits and aspects will take your desires to the ultimate extreme – one way or another. Will you be so fussy in your specifications that you never find anyone who measures up? Or will you be so passionate that you will be looking for a copy of *Kama Sutra Volume 2* after a month?

Venus in Conjunction with White Moon Selena

When Venus meets White Moon Selena it is like the energy of soul mates. You will feel connected to the one you love like they are the missing part of you and you feel as if you are now completely in harmony. Best to be careful because unless the other party has the same conjunction going on, they might not feel the same way about you. Then again you might be lucky enough to meet someone who shares roughly the same birthday as you, a multiple of seven years apart. Then they will be enjoying the same conjunction!

If this conjunction is in your natal chart then you are apt to be on a lifelong quest for your soulmate. If you focus too much on finding the perfect 'Mr Right', you are at risk of missing out on a lot of pleasurable "Mr He'll-do-for-now" romances.

Venus in Opposition to White Moon Selena

When Venus is far away as possible from your White Moon Selena, you may be considering a break-up. Nothing acrimonious, just that you yearn for the simplicity of being by yourself, doing your own thing. You come to feel your relationship (or your search for one, if you are single) is a distraction, pulling you away from where you feel you should be. Don't make a quick decision, look at the pros and cons in a balanced manner before making a move. The feeling might go away as the transit passes.

If this aspect is in your natal chart then you may well be one of nature's confirmed singletons. Your best harmony and balance is within yourself and you believe that a partner, while good for some fun and romance for a while, is only going to unbalance your life in the long run.

Venus Squared with White Moon Selena

"Romance is dead, I'm giving up" is the mantra of Venus when she's squared with White Moon Selena. A history of bad relationships and unrequited loves come to the forefront of your mind at this time. Or you might be going through a bad patch in your present relationship. It is a feeling of 'if it isn't going absolutely right then it must be absolutely wrong'. Your challenge is to realise that harmony is not about everything always being perfect, it is also about how you can make adjustments and compensate to rebalance something that's toppling over.

If this aspect is in your natal chart then you likely wouldn't recognise a soulmate, even if Cupid tied your hearts together with his bowstring. You tend to go for a 'fixer-upper'; completely unsuitable but you are convinced you can change them and make them perfect for you. This holds true for house-restoration as well as romance.

Venus in Trine with White Moon Selena

While Venus is in a very harmonious trine with White Moon Selena, She's in Her element. After all, harmony is one of the energies of Venus. You feel a need to be what you are expected to be, as if it is your responsibility to be the balancing force in any situation. In a relationship, you want to be the perfect partner, fitting in around the needs of your loved one, or intended loved one so they will love you all the more. We all know there is give and take in any relationship, but there is no balance if you are the only one giving.

If this aspect is in your natal chart then you will tend to be a follower rather than a leader. 'Anything for a quiet life' is your mantra when conflict arises and you might come to think that the secret of a perfectly happy relationship is to satisfy your partner's desires more than your own. All well and good if that really makes you happy, but remember, nobody really respects a doormat!

Venus in Sextile with White Moon Selena

During this sextile transit, Venus is stimulated by White Moon Selena to flirt, to romance, to seduce. Whether it is in your work, social or love life, your goal is to be the most wanted and most loved. You want all your best skills on show whenever the boss is around at work. You want your loved one to be dazzled by romantic charm, whether it is by taking them out on an extravagant date or glamming yourself up for a quiet night in. This may work great while it lasts, but how long can you keep it up for before you run out of energy? And your loved one may get suspicious at all this lavish attention; there's a saying "When a man gives his wife flowers for no reason, there's a reason!"

If this aspect is in your natal chart, you have the aptitude to be a flirt and skilled in the art of seduction. You want to be seen as the best you can be. It may make you a true romantic. It may make you a consummate con-artist. Which way will you go?

Mars ♂

Poor Mars can be so misunderstood. The God of War had his glory days in Rome and history has sealed this reputation of being the representation of domination and conquest. But this is doing Him an injustice. Mars was just the energy. It was the Romans who chose to use that Mars energy for power and empire building.

The Greeks understood Him a little better. In the guise of Ares, the God of War was recognised as a force that was part of us; something to be acknowledged and dealt with. But He wasn't worshipped as such. He was stuck at the little table at the back of the pantheon; the embarrassing relative that you have to keep inviting to the party but you don't really like very much.

The Planet Mars is the power of aggression and anger in your chart. And in itself this is no bad thing. As I said, it is a neutral energy that exists within us all and needs to be directed to a purpose. You might use it to fight for power and domination but you might also feel it and use it when you see an injustice being done; seeing a polluted river or homeless people sleeping rough on a winter night. Compassion makes you upset about these things, but it is anger that can make you want to do something about it, to make a positive change. Anger can be a powerful fuel for determination when properly channelled.

Mars orbits the Sun in 687 days, taking just under two months to move through each Sign. So Mars will bump into your natal White Moon Selena fairly often. When this happens, your highest aspirations will feel a renewed focus, one way or another, and a need to make progress to reach your goals. How you act on this focus, with assertive determination or aggression, will depend on the type of aspect.

Mars in Conjunction with White Moon Selena

The drive and determination of Mars focuses your attention on your highest aspirations. You may feel a need to start making a concerted effort towards manifesting your aspirations. All other day-to-day business is going to be put on the back burner now as you become like a moth drawn to a flame. These periodic bursts of energy towards your goal are commendable and will likely be productive but be mindful about what you might be neglecting while you reach for the stars.

Mars in Opposition to White Moon Selena

With Mars now at its furthest distance from White Moon Selena, the frustrations at your divine self being so far away from your reach may boil over into anger with yourself for not living up to your own expectations. You may well pull back and feel like it's no longer worth trying to achieve something that is plainly impossible. As Mars moves on, the feelings will recede and until then you have to remember that it's the striving that's important, not the succeeding.

Mars Squared with White Moon Selena

In the Square aspect, Mars is telling you to give up and look elsewhere. This is the aspect of misdirected determination. Unlike with the Opposition, there is no inward anger. Here your Warrior is just ceding the battleground and feels a calling to a different field that may lead to an easier victory. But is it courageous to only fight a battle you are able to win? Mars will not be satisfied with an easy victory and as it moves away from this aspect it will return to the main war.

Mars in Trine with White Moon Selena

When Mars is in a harmonious trine with White Moon Selena, it feels like the challenge falls away. You no longer see the obstacles in your way and feel that you can make great progress toward achieving your highest aspirations. But you may get complacent with what seems like an easy victory in sight and become like the hare racing the tortoise, distracted and lazy when the challenge seems like a foregone conclusion.

Mars in Sextile with White Moon Selena

When Mars is in sextile with White Moon Selena, you become enthused. The Mars determination and will to advance begins to push you forward. There is a kind of "warrior's madness" or lust for battle that you can become susceptible to. Your Mars-fuelled determination may lead you make great strides forward in your goals. But if your divine goal remains tantalisingly out of reach while this aspect holds, then tempers will be shortened and frustrations grow, the repercussions of which will remain long after Mars has moved on.

Jupiter ♃

Dominating the distant part of the Solar System, ruler of Sagittarius, giant Jupiter is the Planet that 'Coulda' bin a contender!'.

When a body reaches enough mass, a nuclear reaction occurs and it ignites as a star. Jupiter, being more massive than all the rest of the Planets combined, *nearly* made it. But not quite. This big ball of gas has to contend with merely being the biggest fish in its own back 'pond' of the Solar System.

Even in mythology, 'King of the Gods' Jupiter has to deal with the view that He's really a 'supermarket own-brand' Roman knock-off of Zeus.

That is not to say, the Planet Jupiter doesn't have a considerable amount of power and influence itself. According to readings from the Voyager probe, it still manages to shine with more energy than any non-star is expected to. This can mean a bit of unexpected brightness and good fortune in whatever House it is moving through. Look up into a clear night sky and there's no mistaking Jupiter when you spot it; one of the clearest and brightest lights up there.

Jupiter's 12 year orbit will bring it into an aspect with White Moon Selena every couple of years, which is important. It is often enough to give you regular opportunities to assess your progress towards your dreams. White Moon Selena shows us aspirations higher than we are likely to attain and Jupiter is the power that shows us how to cope with failure to live up to over-ambitious goals: with a hearty shrug of the shoulders and a smile on our faces.

Jupiter in Conjunction with White Moon Selena

This hearty meeting of dreams and reality provides an enormous boost to your confidence. It brings you a realisation of exactly how far you might be able to go in your highest aspirations. You know full well that they can never be reached 100%; but 75% or even 80%? That might be doable. Even 50% is pretty good going. It gives you a real kick to feel like you can achieve something tangible.

If this conjunction is in your natal chart then you are not likely the sort of person who sets unreasonable goals. You see your highest aspirations as a series of achievable targets to set your sights upon.

Jupiter in Opposition to White Moon Selena

This tense aspect brings a certain level of stubborn bloody-mindedness to your chart. It tells you that even though you are "fated to fail", you should take the next steps in your journey anyway; if only to prove to yourself and the universe that trying is futile. You can reconcile yourself to failure if you can tell everyone that at least you tried. On the one hand, your fatalism might manifest the failure you are expecting, but sometimes, this pigheadedness works wonders. And nobody will be more surprised than you.

If this aspect is in your natal chart you are apt to be naturally pessimistic and cynical in the face of your dreams. Your challenge is to follow other people's encouragement and adopt a 'nothing to lose by trying' attitude.

Jupiter Squared with White Moon Selena

This fractious aspect brings with it a tendency to give up. Your highest aspirations are never going to be reached. So why make the effort? The challenge here is to channel the energies you do have in a different direction. What Sign and House is your Jupiter in? Does that give you steer as to a new goal to aim for in the meantime? A change is as good as a rest. Spending some time as a gas giant while this aspect is in effect may well refresh you so you can return to your starry aspirations later.

If this aspect is in your natal chart then you are likely to be pulled in both directions. Your Jupiter might be in Taurus, pulling you towards a safe and realistic 9–5 job with 2.5 kids in the suburbs, while your White Moon Selena in Leo is dreaming of breaking out the Fender Stratocaster and taking the band on tour. Your highest aspirations become trying to do a little of both. Secure job during the week and a wild hobby at the weekend, perhaps?

Jupiter in Trine with White Moon Selena

This harmonious aspect brings a peaceful complacency into your journey. You look at your highest aspirations and then sit back and think, "You know what? It really doesn't matter. I can be happy where I am and I shouldn't stress over it." This aspect is tempting you away from making any efforts to strive for your dreams because where you are is good enough. Why strain to be a star if you can be happy as a gas giant? While this trine is in effect, it is fair enough to think of it as a holiday.

If this trine is in your natal chart, you are apt to be satisfied for less than you are capable of reaching. Remember that Sagittarius wants you to appreciate the journey, even if the destination remains a way off.

Jupiter in Sextile with White Moon Selena

This stimulating aspect gives a jump start to your drive to reach your aspirations. If you've not been making much progress in your journey lately, this aspect adds fuel. Where you are headed and how long the journey might be is no longer of any real concern. The only important consideration is Jupiter motivating you out of your armchair and back on the road. An Aquarian Jupiter gives the Sagittarian a new inspiration for the direction of travel. A Taurean Jupiter shows a Piscean how to turn a dream into reality.

If this aspect is in your natal chart then your Jupiter placements will give you added support in how to reach for your highest aspirations. Whether it is by bringing passion to your lofty ideas and learning or giving your fantasies a sense of realism.

Saturn ♄

Saturn, the ruling Planet of Capricorn, is the last of the 'Classical Seven' Planets in astrology and the most distant that it is possible to see with the naked eye. In this way, it has been associated with boundaries and restriction. Not only because it was apparently the boundary of our Solar System, but also because the Planet itself is seemingly restricted by its spectacular system of rings.

In mythology, Saturn is the Roman agricultural god who was the successor to Kronos the Greek Titan, who presided over Order and Time. Taken together, Saturn became the embodiment of time and dedication reaping the rewards.

As Kronos, He was the only child of Gaia that was willing to do the necessary deed of castrating His father, Uranus, and thus releasing Her other children from imprisonment in Tartarus. And later He devoured His own children in fear of a prophesy that one of them would replace Him. These stories exhibit Saturn's qualities of ruthless pragmatism and self-determination.

But there is also an element of this ruthlessness being ultimately self-defeating since He was overthrown by one of His sons, Zeus, in retaliation for eating His other children. Thus Kronos set in motion the events He was trying to prevent.

It is notable that the four quarters of Saturn's 29 year orbit, the squares, the opposition and the eventual return, mark times of significant change in our lives. And each quarter-orbit takes roughly seven years: the period of a White Moon Selena Return heralding a review and reaffirmation of our highest aspirations.

When Saturn comes into an aspect with White Moon Selena, our highest aspirations seem suddenly not so unreachable. They become a challenge to yourself. Because the reality is that Saturn does not form the boundary of our Solar System; there are worlds beyond. You are apt to have faith that with enough focus, hard work and self-discipline, you might break out from apparent restrictions and boundaries and reach your highest aspirations after all.

Saturn in Conjunction with White Moon Selena

This aspect melds the two energies together. Your eye is on the prize. You know what your highest aspirations are and you start to realise that if you apply enough hard work and discipline you can reach them. Your divine self is waiting in front of you and if you can see it you can be it. The danger is that your laser-like focus can make you miss the beautiful breadth of life's experiences.

If this conjunction is in your natal chart, you have a tendency to become very goal oriented; setting targets and making plans to tackle them. On the realisation of your highest aspiration you may well start to plan your life around it.

Saturn in Opposition to White Moon Selena

With this opposition in effect, you may come to realise that hard work and dedication is exactly the *wrong* approach to take if you want to reach your divine self. You feel your aspirations may be impossible to attain by conventional means, so it is time to throw out any logical approach and follow your heart and intuition.

If this opposition is in your natal chart, you would do well to look at where the Moon is or what is happening in your Cancer. Your emotional, instinctive and intuitive forces are what will point to your divine self as Saturn's dogged pragmatic energy is not going to work.

Saturn Squared with White Moon Selena

In this aspect you will feel far too pragmatic to even attempt to reach your highest aspirations. You believe it is impossible so it becomes futile to continue down that path. While this aspect is in effect you may well set your sights on different, lesser ambitions.

If this aspect is in your natal chart then you may have a fairly fatalistic view of life; that no amount of discipline and hard work will take you towards what should be your highest aspirations. To compensate, look to the opposing Sign of Cancer and try to work towards what your gut *feels* is right rather than what you think you *know*.

Saturn in Trine with White Moon Selena

In this harmonious aspect your Saturn will compensate for White Moon Selena's unreachably high aspirations by beginning to set lower targets for yourself. You pragmatically feel that if you can't win the Gold Medal, you could make a decent stab at trying for the Bronze.

If this aspect is in your natal chart you may have a tendency to have low expectations of yourself. You might continually set low targets, already knowing you can achieve them. The result being a lack of motivation to push yourself.

Saturn in Sextile with White Moon Selena

This excitable aspect kicks your self-discipline up a gear with the feelings of self-respect and integrity. It no longer matters to you that you won't achieve your goals, you will shrug and set about it anyway. It becomes a matter of pride to you.

If this aspect is in your natal chart you are one of nature's 'triers'. You enter competitive events and are quite happy to come away with Participation Trophies. You don't play the game because you expect to win, but your strong sense of self-respect demands you try your best.

Uranus

Until 1781, the world of astrology had been well defined for centuries, if not millennia. There were seven Planets in the astrological system and as I said in the introduction chapter, seven was always a very powerful number among many spiritual beliefs and concepts. Then, during this time of great upheaval in the world, (for example, this was the time of the American Revolution), Astrological belief was knocked off its stool by the discovery of a new eighth Planet.

It was absolutely right and just that this supremely awkward new Planet, soon named Uranus, became the ruling Planet of astrology's rebel power, Aquarius. In keeping with this need to be different, it is the only Planet that has an axis that is nearly horizontal rather than the usual vertical. It is also the only one of the Planets to be named after a Greek deity rather than the Roman version (who was called Caelus).

Uranus was the primordial God of the Sky, husband of Gaia and father of the Titans. According to Hesiod's *Theogony,* an 8th century BCE poem about the birth of the gods, Uranus was the first of the gods, either alongside or after Gaia, and had 18 children with Her. He hated his children for reasons that are not clear and hid them away somewhere inside Gaia. (See under *Saturn* for what happened next.) Some accounts suggest that He hid them because they were ugly, but in keeping with the Aquarius/Uranus archetype, I suggest it might have been because He just wanted to be unique.

The orbit of Uranus is 84 years which is 12 times the 7-year orbit of White Moon Selena. This means that White Moon Selena will make one complete cycle while Uranus moves completely through one Sign. Thus all the aspects between Uranus and Selena during one complete cycle, from Conjunction through Squares, Trines,

Sextile and Opposition, will generally happen while Uranus is under the influence of one single Sign.

When Uranus is in an aspect with White Moon Selena, the usual effect is a sense of going it alone. If this is difficult, invoke Leo, the opposing Sign to Aquarius. Send up a beacon of light to allow the people around you to see you and know that you need their support.

Uranus in Conjunction with White Moon Selena

When Uranus meets White Moon Selena it brings a feeling of uniqueness to your highest aspirations. You feel that you might be the only person ever who has striven for this goal. Or at least the only one who might achieve it. This feeling will give you a sense of purpose for the time this Conjunction is felt and an extra boost on your journey.

If this aspect is in your natal chart, you may have a sense of being special; that your highest aspirations might be your special destiny (have a look where your Pluto is to see if it feeds into this sense).

Uranus in Opposition to White Moon Selena

With Uranus opposing White Moon Selena you may feel competitive in striving for your highest aspirations. A nagging feeling arises that someone else might get there and prevent you from doing so. Depending on what Signs are in action here, this could bring a feeling of defeat (if White Moon Selena is in a Water Sign, for example) or you may be spurred faster onwards to 'win the race' (if your White Moon Selena is in a Fire Sign).

If this aspect is in your natal chart you are apt to be competitive. Your sense of uniqueness leads you to believe there can be only one who wins the gold medal.

Uranus Squared with White Moon Selena

This normally fractious aspect may be to your advantage. You may feel the pull of being the lone wolf in this journey to your highest aspirations but you know that being a team player is going to work better for you at this stage. Uranus is working against you so be collaborative. Seek and accept all help and advice.

If this aspect is in your natal chart you may feel that you are never going to get anywhere in life, especially not reaching your highest aspirations, by yourself. You tend to get further by building a support network to keep you on track.

Uranus in Trine with White Moon Selena

This harmonious aspect brings with it a sense of loneliness. Being unique can be synonymous with being alone and that there is nobody around you that you can turn to for help in striving for your highest aspirations. This is not, of course, likely to be true, but it is a difficult feeling to deal with and you might miss opportunities for help that is out there.

If this aspect is in your natal chart you may feel inclined to be self-sufficient in your goal setting; that you are more comfortable striving for your highest aspirations by yourself. You tend to feel more satisfaction knowing you have achieved things without help. Your mantra in this respect becomes "if you want a job done properly, do it yourself!"

Uranus in Sextile with White Moon Selena

This excitable aspect brings with it a realisation that the only reason why your highest aspirations are unreachable is because you simply haven't found the right method yet. You tend to feel that all you need to reach them is to come up with a radically new approach that nobody has ever tried before. Whether this requires a touch of genius or madness is open to interpretation. But if, say, your highest aspiration was to be a world renowned chef, it is under this aspect that you might create a monstrosity like, as comedian Jeremy Hardy once proposed, "liver meringue pie" in the hope it will catch on!

If this aspect is in your natal chart then you may well embody the archetype of 'mad scientist'. You are most likely to become an inventor or experimenter. You might end up as the next Steve Jobs. You might win the Nobel Prize. Or you might end up blowing up your garden shed while building a better mousetrap!

Neptune

Ψ

Neptune is our gateway to the divine and the magical. Whenever one of our Planets moves into aspect with Neptune, there is a mystical spark. Our imagination comes alive with new possibilities and insight. On the other hand, it can also lead us into delusions. It is the ruling Planet of Pisces and thus connects us with the dreams, fantasies and illusions that reside in the depths of our souls.

When Neptune is in an aspect with White Moon Selena, we are hit with what can only be viewed as a Divine revelation. Our insight goes within and we see ourselves how the Divine sees us.

It is not something that happens often. Neptune has an orbit of 165 years. That works out at nearly 14 years in each Sign, on average. If you are lucky, you might see one occasion of Neptune transiting your natal Selena. (It happens to me in about 20 years' time if I live long enough to see it, but as I will have just had my 11th Selena Return, I probably won't have too many high aspirations for the future by then!)

But even if Neptune never meets your natal White Moon Selena in your lifetime, there is still the similar impact of the seven yearly meeting of White Moon Selena with your natal Neptune to consider.

Neptune in Conjunction with White Moon Selena

The magical insight of Neptune allows the divine calling of White Moon Selena to be perceived and understood with complete clarity. It's as if the doorway to your Heaven has opened and the Divine is showing you your best and highest self. Allow yourself to hear it and you will know with no doubt what you are meant to be.

If this conjunction is in your natal chart then throughout your life you will believe in your calling and your ability to achieve it (whether you actually have that ability is neither here nor there).

Neptune in Opposition to White Moon Selena

It is in this aspect that doubt enters your soul. It is a crisis of faith that tries to convince you that you are wrong in your aspirations. Here, Neptune is farthest away from the influence of White Moon Selena and is pulling you away from Her. Her voice is obscured by delusion and you will be tempted down different, less fulfilling and possibly darker paths.

If this opposition is in your natal chart then it will be more difficult to believe in your calling but that need not stop you. White Moon Selena will make Herself known some other way.

Neptune Squared with White Moon Selena

Neptune as a square brings a different kind of doubt. It is the crisis of confidence in yourself, creating the delusion that it is not worth striving for something you are never going to attain. Neptune will lead you to believe you are meant for lesser things because that's all you are good for. The challenge is to remember that it doesn't matter if you don't attain your goal. The point is to try.

If this Square is in your natal chart then a lack of confidence is often going to plague you. But this is one of Neptune's delusions; a lack of confidence does not mean a lack of ability.

Neptune in Trine with White Moon Selena

The harmonic energy of the trine with Neptune brings a belief in yourself that all things are possible. You are filled with faith that you actually can reach and achieve your highest aspiration. It is not a matter of confidence in your abilities, it more that you believe there is a destiny that is leading you there if you keep the faith. Faith and belief can be a tremendous boost, but never forget that Neptune's power can be illusionary as well as magical. And, crucially in astrology, like all Planets, it is also transitory. Over-confidence and self-delusion are the greatest dangers during this transit.

If this trine is in your natal chart then you are likely to have a strong belief that your highest aspirations are your destiny. Your challenge is to temper your confidence with common sense and remember that you generally have to put the work in if you are to achieve anything.

Neptune in Sextile with White Moon Selena

This aspect brings the energy of encouragement and excitement. Neptune's stimulation of the imagination will help you believe that all things are possible. But unlike with the trine aspect, here it brings insight into how you need to make it possible. You are not trusting to divine will and pure faith alone, you will come to imagine you do have, or can gain, the abilities required to reach your highest aspiration. As it often is with White Moon Selena, it may still turn out to be beyond your means, but at least you are more likely to work towards it and achieve something.

If this sextile is in your natal chart then you are likely to have a strong belief in yourself and your soul's inner resources.

Pluto

P

We finally reach what is one of the outermost major bodies of our Solar System. Out there in the darkness, named after the God of the Underworld; so mysterious we can't even decide whether it is a proper planet or not. It's definition keeps changing. Since 2006 it has been classed as a 'dwarf planet' along with several other similar size 'Trans-Neptune' and Asteroid Belt bodies.

With an elliptical and tilted orbit of 248 years, it moves slowly and irregularly through the Zodiac, bringing generational upheavals in its wake. It entered Capricorn in 2008 at the time of the great banking collapses in the West and is now moving, in 2024, into Aquarius for the first time since the American and French Revolutions.

Its placement in our charts confronts us with our power in the face of destiny. When Pluto comes into an aspect with White Moon Selena we are faced with how our divine selves impact the people and world around us. Are we at the forefront of evolution or as insignificant as a distant sunbeam seen from Pluto's surface?

Pluto in Conjunction with White Moon Selena

When these two powerful energies meet, aspirations meet destiny. This is your moment to stand up and be counted. It is time to do something to make the world sit up and take notice. Are you going to write that song that will go triple-platinum? Do you feel called to put your name forward in an election? Am I going to write a book that takes the astrology world by storm? Is your highest aspiration something that the world will remember you for?

If this aspect is in your natal chart then you may feel that you are a child of destiny. Your highest aspirations are likely to be ones that will impact society around you rather than be personal.

Pluto in Opposition to White Moon Selena

When White Moon Selena pulls far away from Pluto you turn your back on destiny. This is not to say that becoming your divine self would have no impact, but for the time this aspect is in operation, your motives behind striving for your highest aspirations turn inward. Spend this time considering the impact it is having on you alone, as opposed to the world around you.

If this aspect is in your natal chart then your highest aspirations are more likely to be personal, affecting only you and your immediate circle. Any impact you care to have on society as a whole will be negligible at best.

Pluto Squared with White Moon Selena

In this fractious aspect with Pluto, you may feel a sense that the world around you is actively holding you back from becoming your divine self. This may be simple paranoia or maybe the world really is out to get you. Either way, you will feel held back. It might be a good time to consider how people would react or respond to you if you did become your divine self. Be prepared for it.

If this aspect is in your natal chart then you may find yourself at odds with society at large. You strive to move away from the tide of history. If the world seems more joined up by technology, for example, your highest aspirations will prosper more in an analogue environment.

Pluto in Trine with White Moon Selena

This harmonious aspect brings the power of allies to your side. You are striving towards aspirations that society around you tends to share. The challenge with this harmony is to ensure your aspirations are not being diluted to a lowest common denominator in order to fit in with the movement of the crowd.

If this aspect is in your natal chart then your highest aspirations tend to drift along the flow of history, feeling a pull to fit in with a collective movement rather than be an expression of your own individuality.

Pluto in Sextile with White Moon Selena

As with the Trine aspect above, the Sextile aspect will also attract allies. But in this case they are more likely to support your goals than expect you to adapt to theirs. When you strive towards your highest aspirations you appear as a light out of the darkness to those around you and will rally to your cause.

If this aspect is in your natal chart then your highest aspirations will likely lead you to be an influencer in your community. Show you are striving for the benefit of their development and you will likely find all the support you need.

The Ascendant

I mentioned the Ascendant earlier in Chapter 4 in the description of the First House. It isn't a planetary body or even any kind of astronomical virtual point in the sky. It is actually the Eastern horizon.

Your Ascendant is the Sign that is appearing and rising in the sky over the Eastern horizon at the time you were born. It is also called your 'Rising Sign'. All twelve Houses are measured from this horizon and the 'Planetary' qualities of the Ascendant are associated with the First House.

I include it here because it is one of the 'big three' in astrological measurement. The majority of our astrological make-up comes from the Sun Sign (core identity), the Moon Sign (emotional responses) and the Ascendant (outward personality).

This is our public face, the way we like to be seen around friends, workmates and sometimes even family. We don't always wear our hearts on our sleeves or bare the full true depths of our souls when we are out in the streets. We put on a mask of personality in the same way as we put on our clothes.

In an astrology reading, we consider aspects to the Ascendant in the same way as we consider aspects to any other Planet. In considering aspects to the Ascendant we naturally end up considering the Descendant on the Western horizon, Midheaven at the height of the sky and the Nadir on the opposite side of the world too. However they have a lesser impact in themselves and specific examinations of their aspects is outside the scope of this book.

In White Moon Selena's seven-year journey around the chart, the following transiting aspects are likely to be felt for six to seven weeks.

White Moon Selena in Conjunction with the Ascendant

In this aspect you are likely to be very open about your highest aspirations, inviting people around to see you as you want them to see you, not necessarily as you are. You are, in effect, pretending to be your divine self ahead of time, giving the world a preview of all you could be.

If this aspect is in your natal chart then your White Moon Selena is in your First House and your self-development progress is most likely a public performance. You make no secret of your aspirations and the more you show it, you reason, the closer you are to becoming it.

White Moon Selena in Opposition to the Ascendant

In this opposing aspect, White Moon Selena is on your Descendant, the entry point of the Seventh House. The emphasis is less on you and more on those close to you. It becomes important to consider whether those close to you are attracted to the person you are or the potential they imagine your divine self to be. There may be a temptation to live up to their expectations, not your own true path.

If this aspect is in your natal chart, then your White Moon Selena is in your Seventh House and your personality is likely to take on the traits of the person closest to you, mirroring that person who you view as the other half of your soul. This is all very well if it truly is your Seventh House soulmate but otherwise, you could run the risk of suppressing your core self and risking your own mental health in the long run by pretending to be someone you are not. If you think this is happening, look at your Sun Sign, read the relevant section about it in Chapter 6 or even take cues from your daily horoscope in the morning newspaper. Lean in to the archetypes of both your

Sun Sign and your Ascendant, like taking up a competitive sport if you are an Aries, for example, and re-establish your core self and personal sovereignty.

White Moon Selena Squared with the Ascendant

In this aspect, as with the Opposition, there is a pull to align your Divine Self potential with the outer world. This will differ, depending on whether the Square is on the Midheaven above or the Nadir below.

If White Moon Selena is on the Midheaven, the entry point of the Tenth House, you may feel a temporary fear that the outside world is not going to accept your Divine Self and inhibit your progress towards your highest aspirations.

If White Moon Selena is on the Nadir, the entry point to the Fourth House, then it may well be family pressures or your living environment that is temporarily inhibiting you from showing your highest aspirations.

If this aspect is in your natal chart then you may be inclined to keep your highest aspirations a secret from the outside world or family, depending on which Square it is. This does not necessarily have to have an effect on your highest aspirations, you just might prefer to keep quiet about them and work towards them in your own way.

White Moon Selena in Trine with the Ascendant

In this harmonious aspect, your White Moon Selena is not on a horizon or meridian, but it is in the same element as the Ascendant. You are likely to feel quite comfortable in your Divine skin and how people perceive you is not really that important. You feel a sense that you know who you are and what you can become, and the rest of the world can keep their opinions to themselves.

If this aspect is in your natal chart then you tend to show a sense of relaxed self-assuredness about your highest aspirations. You may have an appearance of self-confidence that you can stroll purposefully towards becoming your Divine Self without worrying about what anyone else thinks.

White Moon Selena in Sextile with the Ascendant

In this stimulating aspect, your White Moon Selena is not on a horizon or meridian, but it is in a supporting element to that of the Ascendant. For this period, you may be feeling very keen to make a public display of your aspirations, making it known and obvious to the world where you see yourself going. This level of openness may be something you need, to help give yourself a push in your development.

If this aspect is in your natal chart then your general outward personality is likely to be enhanced by a touch of the Divine. Those around you are more likely to perceive the potential in you rather than how you are at the moment.

8. The White Moon Selena Return

It's my 56th birthday and a couple of days ago I was lying in bed awake, waiting for a 3am alarm to go off for a long bus journey. I spent those early hours musing over various aspects of White Moon Selena when it suddenly hit me what being 56 would mean: it was my 8th Selena Return.

A Return is when a Planet's orbit brings it back to the same position it was in at your birth. This conjunction can be one of the most personally powerful types of transit. The most well known in astrology is the Saturn Return, every 28–29 years, which heralds significant life changes (and yes, I'm acutely aware that I've got my second Saturn Return coming in the next couple of years!)

The White Moon Selena Return is unique amongst transits (apart from the Solar Return, obviously!) in that it always occurs on (or very near) your birthday, due to Selena's impossibly perfect and precise orbit.

So what does the Selena Return herald?

White Moon Selena is the divine pull in our lives and so when 'She returns to us', so to speak, it can become a dedication ritual. It's our opportunity to reconnect with our highest aspirations. Either to reconfirm them and rededicate ourselves, or more likely to discover new ones. Our highest aspirations are not static throughout our lives. The Sign and House White Moon Selena appears in on our natal charts may point to those areas of our lives in which our highest aspirations will be directed, but the specifics will shift and evolve as we grow (After all, at my first Selena Return in 1975, my highest aspiration was to be an astronaut!)

We can find clues into what direction our aspirations could take in this next White Moon Selena orbit by looking at what Planets are in aspect to White Moon Selena at the moment of the transit.

I like to adapt existing, long-standing traditions and rituals in my work. It adds a greater resonance to the ceremony. So a rededication ceremony on my White Moon Selena Return Birthday would be to have a round birthday cake, covered with Moonlike white icing, and blow out the candles. In this case, it would be eight candles to represent the completion of eight cycles of White Moon Selena on my 56th birthday. It extinguishes the illumination of the old versions of our highest aspirations as we 'make a wish' for our new version to manifest. We absorb the representative energies of the eight White Moon Selena cycles by eating the cake (an arduous ritual, but it has to be done.) Finally we can light a brand new candle to honour the beginning of the next cycle.

9. Putting It All Together – The Case Studies

In the following case studies I will first be looking at the primal triad of Sun, Moon and Ascendant placements in the subjects' natal charts. Between those three we get a fairly rounded summary of who they are: their core, true self, their emotional soul responses and their surface personality they project to the world. I will stick to the triad unless there is another Planet with a very significant placement.

Looking then at their White Moon Selena placements, with all prominent planetary aspects, will show them a highest divine self that they might aspire to become. I say 'a' rather than 'the' because there are obviously many mountains one can climb in life and there may well be a different variant of 'highest' self on each peak. The White Moon Selena energy is, in effect, a divination message through the Portal from the spiritual realms as to the highest potential their Divine Powers would direct them towards.

The reading does not predict whether their highest aspirations are fully attainable. Nor does it describe what they should do in order to progress towards it (although some more clues may be found in a deep dive into the natal charts and current or future transits). But it does indicate some paths to take and possible challenges to take on.

The Sagittarian

Meet C. She's a 32 year old Sagittarian approaching the end of a period of study.

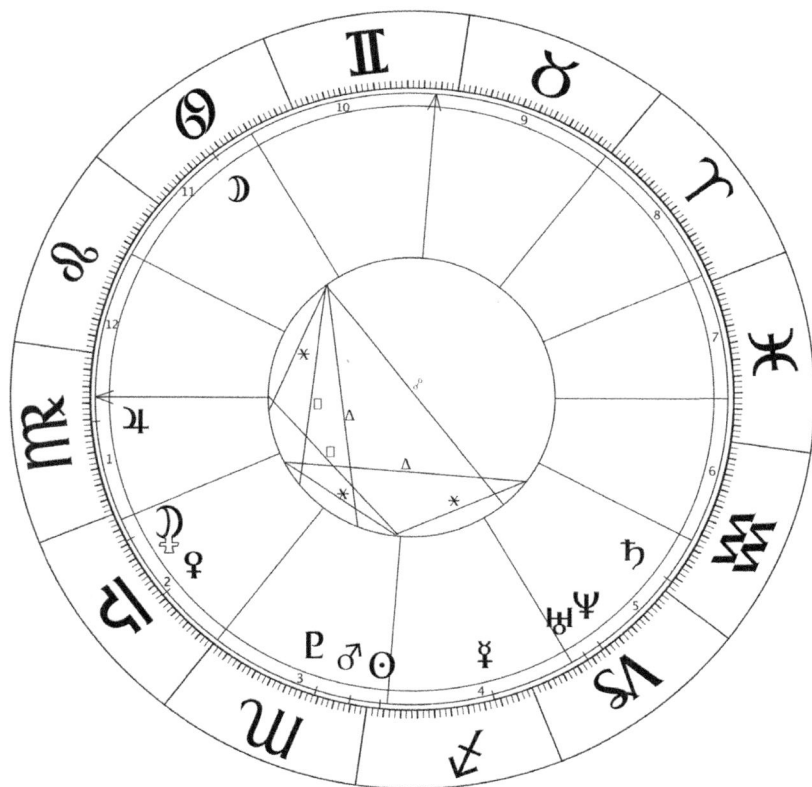

Her Sun is 3rd House Sagittarius which speaks to a strong creative urge and it is in Sextile with Saturn which infuses her creativity with a useful shot of ruthless self-discipline. Her Sun is also in Sextile with White Moon Selena but I'll come back to that later.

Her Moon is in 11th House Cancer. The Moon is, of course, the ruling Planet of Cancer so the emotional sensitivity is double-downed. She is going to be very community minded with her moods fluctuating according to how she views her position amongst her peers. Her Moon is in an incredibly active position, Opposing Neptune, Squared with Venus, and to a lesser extent, in Trine with Pluto and Sextile with Jupiter. Taken together, she may be insightful but uncomfortable with her self-image and feel pressured to always put on a caring sweet face for her community.

Her Ascendant is in Virgo, bringing a sense of devotion and service. This fits well with her Moon placements, but her Ascendant is also Square with the Sun which brings a conflict between who she is and who she feels she is compelled to be in her community.

To sum up, C is an insightful and focused creative person who would love nothing better than to offer her skills to her community but tends to feel undervalued with a pressure to conform to their expectations.

Now, C's White Moon Selena is in 2nd House Libra, in Sextile with the Sun and in Trine with Saturn.

Libra brings a need for harmony and balance as her highest aspiration. Her life's central conflict is her need to serve in her own way, making the best use of her skills as opposed to her community wanting her to conform to their needs. The resolution of this conflict is in showing her community that what they need most from her is precisely what she wants to offer.

Her 2nd House placement shows that the key to resolution is the need to prove herself. She needs to successfully be in balance between herself and her community in order to *prove* to herself that she *can* successfully be in balance between herself and her community. It is the paradox of the effect coming before the cause.

However, where logic fails in being able to resolve this paradox, intuitive leaps can cross the threshold. C's White Moon Selena is in Sextile with the Sun bringing all the power of her imagination and creativity. Her Sagittarian Sun already can see clearly beyond that paradox threshold. Using her creative skills to craft a clear image of her highest aspirations, serving her community on her own terms, will provide the boost she needs to demonstrate 2nd House proof of her divine identity.

C's challenge comes from the White Moon Selena Trine with her Aquarian Saturn. While this Saturn helps in providing ingenious solutions to obstacles, it also brings a counterproductive tendency to make pragmatic compromises in order to achieve partial victories. She must take the genius influence to boost the Sextile Sun's effect but resist the pull to compromise her ideals or she will be back at the beginning.

In three years, C will reach her 5th Selena Return. This will put White Moon Selena in Opposition with the Ariean Saturn and, to a lesser extent, Neptune and in Trine with Pluto and Uranus. These Oppositions could bring doubt that her hard work is getting anywhere. The Trine with Uranus may well make her feel that she is having to cope alone but that is when the Aquarian Pluto Trine can redress the balance and bring the community to her side. It is her own unique insights, wisdom and imagination that will make the difference. With these aspects, it is likely that people will listen and stand at C's side on her terms.

C answers:

"Wow this really resonates for me. A lot of situations in my life that have resulted in inner conflict have been rooted in me vs. the community, whether that's a group of friends or family. I have

compromised my own desires a lot in my early life, conforming to what friends wanted from me and what my parents expected from me. I can even see this reflected in my spiritual community, which I have recently been questioning my involvement in. I know I have people pleasing tendencies and I do usually end up compromising my own desires in order to keep the peace. This has been very enlightening information. I know now what needs to be done with regards to the current conflict between my desires and the expectations my spiritual community puts on me."

The Gemini

Meet E. She's a 52 year old Gemini, widowed a few years ago and struggling to build a new life for herself.

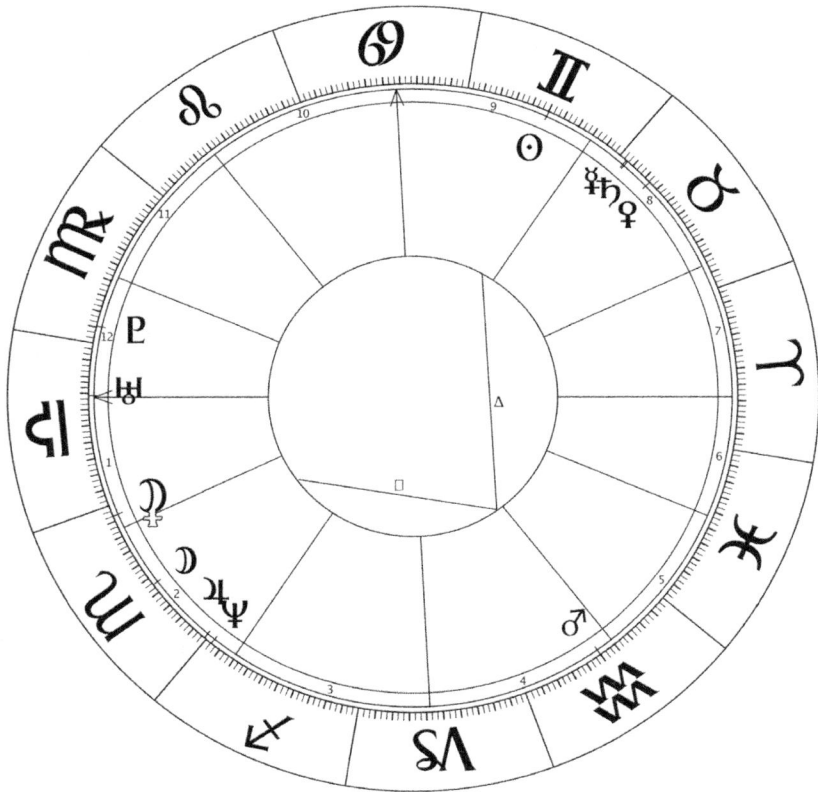

Her Sun is 9th House Gemini. This indicates a tendency to be impulsive and impatient; eager for excitement and experience. Her Sun is in Trine with an Aquarian Mars, adding to her eagerness with an outspoken directness and vitality.

E's Moon is in 2nd House Scorpio which makes her form very deep emotional attachments and invests a lot of her self-esteem in having such attachments. Because of this, her Moon being Square with Mars can leave her very unsatisfied when she is not able to take the initiative in relationships.

Her Ascendant is in Libra, conjunct with Uranus which indicates a daily struggle to bring a sense of peace and balance to her restless nature; that any stresses need to be dealt with in a continuous game of 'whack-a-mole'.

To sum up, she is a dynamic, forthright person who may feel a strong need for deep passionate relationships to feel complete and at peace with herself.

White Moon Selena comes into E's life in 1st House Scorpio which is a perfect blend of self-awareness and self-development. Her divine self is a person who knows how to be complete in herself and is fully aware how to resolve all traumas in her life. And when she's 'got it' she is happy to flaunt it! She has no need to compromise; she wants the world to see her as she is. It does not change or negate her *desire* for a passionate relationship but would reduce the emotional *need* for one.

There are no Planets in any aspect with her White Moon Selena. It is her 1st House placement which points the way to how to strive towards her divine self. It is through the development of self-care as opposed to seeking fulfilment through a partner.

Three years ago, on her 7th Selena Return, E's White Moon Selena was Square with Aquarius Saturn and a weak Opposition with Uranus. Combined they would dampen down her will to develop and look after herself and make her feel unable to do so.

When she hits her 8th Return on turning 56, her White Moon Selena will be Square with Aquarius Pluto and in Trine with Cancerian Mercury. This is likely to lead her to decide to take on the world, lowering her defences and taking action to make herself noticed and wanted.

E answers:

"The first part is pretty accurate although I can be overly polite & 'English' as well as being outspoken & direct. I think I was pretty detached & thoughtless quite frankly about relationships up until relatively recently. It's only fairly recently that I have completely changed from totally career oriented & self-esteem pinned to that only to someone who then began to love far far deeper & to feel & empathise with others. Basically a personality change! Unfortunately (or fortunately), I have totally rejected seeking fulfilment via my own self. This, however, was the way that I WAS for many, many years."

The Taurean

Meet L. He's a 20 year old student in his first year away from home.

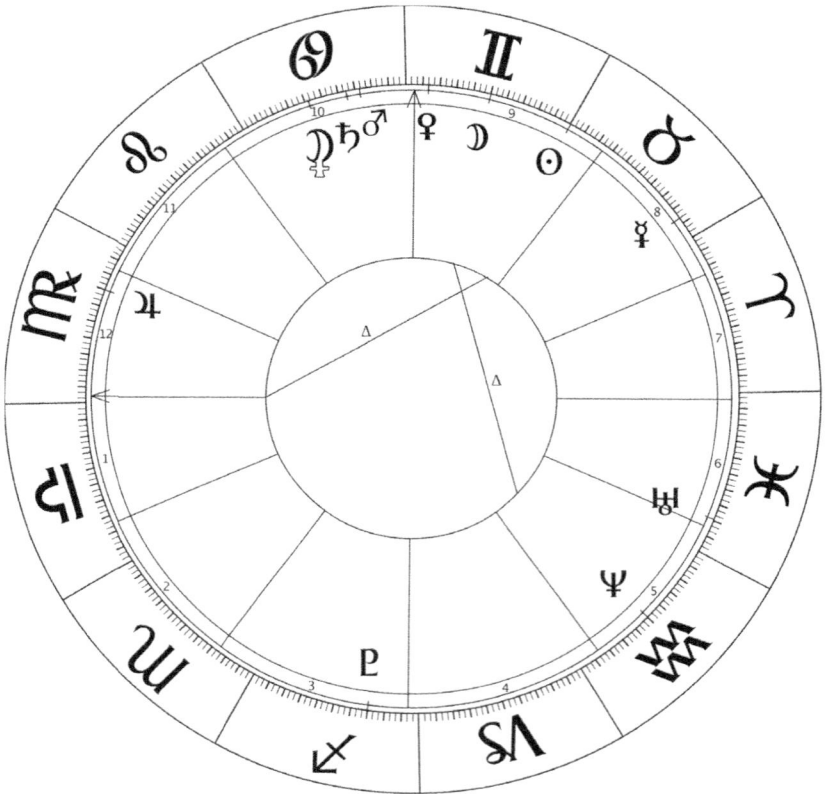

His Sun is 9th House Taurus. This brings a relaxed outlook, which is centred around his creature comforts. The 9th House suggests a 'wherever I lay my hat' approach to life but he will like to make sure it is a comfortable and cozy 'hat'. His Sun is Trine with his Virgo Ascendant which gives him a strong-willed and stubborn 'what you see is what you get' persona; his external Virgo personality being in harmony with his Taurean identity.

His Moon is in 9th House Gemini, in Trine with Aquarian Neptune which can make him a sensitive, but imaginative dreamer who, again, might not be comfortable settling in one place for too long.

White Moon Selena enters L's life in 10th House Cancer with no aspects in play. It brings a strong need for recognition and a high status in his chosen field. But the 10th House is associated with Capricorn, the opposite Sign to Cancer so this opposing factor, along with L's tendency to feeling unsettled, may make it difficult for him to determine what his chosen field might be.

There is a pull towards doing what is expected rather than doing what he truly needs to do. The Taurean in him may well prefer to adopt that approach for the benefit of an easy life. If he does excel at doing what the people around him want him to do then he will indeed enjoy recognition and status, but it may well not be as satisfying as he would imagine.

His next Selena Return, in two years, sees White Moon Selena in Sextile with Taurean Mercury and Squared with Arian Venus. This is likely to enable him to find his niche. Whether it is an area he has chosen or a path he has been directed down, he will likely discover an aspect of it to grasp onto and make his own with enthusiastic gusto. But he should be wary not to let everything else completely fall by the wayside.

10. Where Do We Go From Here?

By now, I hope you will understand your White Moon Selena Sign and House placement. This is showing you which part of your life offers you the path to your highest aspirations and helps you understand the most natural approach you take to reach them.

And by understanding how the constant transiting movement of the Planets every day can affect our attitudes, confidence and vision of our evolution to our Divine Selves, you will be able to recognise a crisis of confidence or faith in yourself when it comes; or the days when the Planets are giving you a boost.

Either way, you can now plan for it and either take advantage by riding with the flow, hunker down and sit it out until the transit passes, or use some of the astrological techniques described in the relevant sections to compensate for the effect.

We still might never fully reach our highest aspirations and actually become our Divine Selves. But few people genuinely do. And that is not really the point. It is our growth and evolution towards that ultimate potential that counts; what we accomplish on the journey rather than reaching the destination.

Understanding what White Moon Selena is showing us and pointing us towards will help us make that journey easier and get much further along that path than we otherwise might.

If you wish to take it to the next level, I invite you to contact me for a personal astrology reading.

In a personal session we will examine your whole birth chart with emphasis on what White Moon Selena is pointing you towards in order to reach your Divine Self, connecting with your god/goddess within.

We will work with your birth chart and transit charts to establish strategies and techniques to help you:

- identify your Ascendant and Houses if you don't know your time of birth;
- move forward along the path to manifesting your Divine Self;
- identify and deal with obstacles that have been holding you back from fulfilling your greater purpose;
- cope positively with reaching for what might be unreachable; and
- chart a pattern through your past, present and future via your Selena Returns.

You will also receive your own personal *Enlightenment of Sound* meditation CD or download of a Planetary Soundscapes crystal bowl soundbath, using the planetary tone of White Moon Selena harmonised with the tones of its aspecting Planets. Listening to the tones of the Planets in a meditative setting helps you integrate their energies within your body, thus helping you grow in harmony with the messages of your birth chart.

Book your session (available either in person, if possible, or on video call) at www.heavensmoon.co.uk

You can also find details of when I will be holding talks or workshops, where we can work with the energies of White Moon Selena in groups.

I look forward to working with you on this journey.

11. References and Bibliography

Baldwin, J. (1961). The New Lost Generation, *Esquire*, (July 1961 Volume LVI, Number 1), New York: Esquire Inc

Blackwood, D. (2023). *The Twelve Faces of the Goddess,* Woodbury: Llewellyn publications

Bukurova, A. V. (2021). Heritage Of Cultural Traditions In Modern Astrology. In D. K. Bataev, et al (Eds.), Knowledge, Man and Civilization – ISCKMC 2020, vol 107. *European Proceedings of Social and Behavioural Sciences* (pp. 274–280). European Publisher. Available from https://doi.org/10.15405/epsbs.2021.05.37 [Accessed 18 March 2024]

Crockford, S. (2018). A Mercury Retrograde Kind of Day: Exploring Astrology in Contemporary New Age Spirituality and American Social Life, *Correspondences*, Volume 6 (no. 1), 47–75. Available from www.researchgate.net/publication/330651010_A_Mercury_Retrograde_Kind_of_Day_Exploring_Astrology_in_Contemporary_New_Age_Spirituality_and_American_Social_Life [Accessed 20 March 2024]

Faulks, D. (2016). *Additional Symbols for Astrology, Revised* [*L2/16-080R*]. Unicode Technical Committee. Available from https://unicode.org/L2/L2016/16080r-add-astrology.pdf [Accessed 18 March 2024]

Forrest, S. (2012). *The Inner Sky: How to Make Wise Choices for a Fulfilling Life,* 3rd Ed. Borrego Springs: Seven Paws Press

Globa, P. P. (2001). *Special Positions of the Planets.* Minsk, ASTRA.

Hone, M. E. (1978). *The Modern Text-Book of Astrology,* 3rd Ed. Romford: L. N. Fowler & Co. Ltd.

Hughes, B. (2019). *Mars Uncovered: Ancient God of War,* BBC Four, 25 March, 9pm

Lineman, R. and Popelka, J. (1984). *Compendium of Astrology,* Gloucester: Para Research Inc

Jones, M. (2023). Handouts and Study Materials Received in the Silver Spiral Star Priest/ess Training. Glastonbury Goddess Temple. www.stellarmysteryschool.com

Jones, P. (1991). *Creative Astrology: Experiential Understanding of the Horoscope,* London: The Aquarian Press

Kaldera, R (2009). *Pagan Astrology,* Rochester: Destiny Books

Keats, J (2008). *The Project Gutenberg eBook of Endymion: A Poetic Romance,* London: Taylor and Hessey. Available from www.gutenberg.org/files/24280/24280-h/24280-h.htm [Accessed 13 April 2024]

Koch, D. and Dr Treindl, A. (2022). *Swiss Ephemeris: Computer Ephemeris For Developers of Astrological Software,* version 2.10.03. Zurich: Astrodienst. Available from www.astro.com/swisseph/swisseph.htm [Accessed 20 January 2024]

Lucian of Samosata. [translated by Hickes, F.] (2014). *The Project Gutenberg eBook of Lucian's True History*, London: A. H. Mullen. Available from www.gutenberg.org/ebooks/45858 [Accessed 13 April 2024]

Meel, S (2017). Fictitious Planets: Black Moon Lilith & White Moon Arta, a*stro-kitty.com.* Available from https://web.archive.org/web/20190310124044/https://astro-kitty.com/black-moon-lilith-white-moon-arta/ [Accessed 24 March 2024]

Moore, S (2011). *Somnium.* London: Strange Attractor Press

Moore, A (2012). *Unearthing,* Marietta: Top Shelf Productions

Moore, S. (2023). *Selene: The Moon Goddess and Cave Oracle,* 2nd Ed. London: Strange Attractor Press

Müller, F. M. (1885). [translated by various] *The Sacred Books of the East,* Volume 24, Oxford: Clarendon Press

Peters, F. K. (2022). *Reclaim Your Dark Goddess,* New South Wales: Rockpool Publishing

Plato [translated by Jowett, B.] (2009). *The Socratic Dialogues (Kaplan Classics of Law)*, Kaplan Trade

Revilla, J. A. (2003). The Astronomical Variants of the Lunar Apogee – Black Moon. *Guías Costa Rica – Expreso.* Available from https://web.archive.org/web/20190313183902/https://expreso.co.cr/centaurs/blackmoon/barycentric.html [Accessed 24 March 2024]

sentinel1x (2022). Of Crosses and White Moons, r/ NewEsotericAstrology. *reddit*. Available from www.reddit.com/r/ NewEsotericAstrology/comments/rnp7cv/of_crosses_and_white_ moons/ [Accessed 18 March 2024]

Stone, A. (2011). Lunar Rover: An Interview With Steve Moore, *The Quietus*. Available from https://thequietus.com/articles/07629-steve-moore-interview-somnium [Accessed 3 May 2024]

Stausberg, M. & Tessmann, A. (2013). The appropriation of a religion: The case of Zoroastrianism in contemporary Russia. *Culture and Religion*, 14(4), 445–462. Available from https://doi.org/10.1080/1475 5610.2013.838800 [Accessed 1 May 2024]

Timashev, A. (1996). Ephemerides of the True Light Moon, *The Russian Professional Astrology*. Available from https://astrologer. ru/book/light_moon/index.html.en. [Accessed 18 March 2024]

Zaehner, R. C. (1998). Iranian Religions: Zurvânism: The Religion of Zurvan, the God of Infinite Time and Space, *The Circle of Ancient Iranian Studies (CAIS)*. Available from www.cais-soas.com/CAIS/ Religions/iranian/zurvanism.htm [Accessed 7 April 2024]

Unless noted above, all other Classical Era sources referenced in the text were to be found in Steve Moore's *Selene: The Moon Goddess and Cave Oracle*.

About the Author

David T Spofforth is a Priest of Avalon, initiated at the Glastonbury Goddess Temple in 2010, and since then has trained and worked in Soul and Sound Healing, Tarot and Goddess-Centred Astrology.

He is also a Priest of Isis with a London Iseum of the Fellowship of Isis and has worked as a Pagan Chaplain in London for over a decade.

From 2011 to 2016 he served on The Pagan Federation National Committee, representing the PF on radio and television, and was publisher of *Pagan Dawn* magazine. Subsequently he continued with the magazine on tours of duty as editor, designer and contributor.

He creates and performs astrological & planetary sound baths as "Enlightenment of Sound" in London and Glastonbury and offers White Moon Selena based astrological consultations and healing.

And he has been known to put paintbrush to canvas on occasion, whenever inspiration hits.

He is an Aquarius with his White Moon Selena in 10th House Taurus... Now you've read the book, you can draw your own conclusions!

Links:

www.heavensmoon.co.uk

www.enlightenmentofsound.co.uk
www.instagram.com/enlightenmentofsound
www.facebook.com/enlightenmentofsound

Printed in Great Britain
by Amazon

50079422R00086